Mama Raised Me,

GOD MADE ME

My Life...My Story

Book Written By:

R.L. SMITH

FOREWORD

I never thought in all my years that I would become an author. It's a true blessing not to just share my story with you all; but to inspire, bring hope, and encourage you to become the person that God made you to be. The thing that you have to always remember is this; God has a plan and purpose for your life. There is no mistake that you're here on Earth. In order to find your divine purpose, you must seek Him.

Remember this, finding your purpose is not about satisfying yourself or being about you. It's more about what God wants to do through you. I pray that when you read this book, your purpose will be shown to you like it was shown to me.

I want to say God Bless you in a mighty way and I hope I get to hear from you in the near future.

DEDICATION

I'm dedicating this book to my Lord and savior Jesus Christ, the true living God. This book was created to not only share wisdom and insight on who Jesus Christ truly is, but to share with you my personal testimony and my walk with Christ in this journey. I have to say that nothing brings me so much joy than to see others pursue their God-given purpose. This book also serves as a guide to help those that have been put down, shunned, neglected, rejected, or feel like there is truly no hope.

I'm here to say that with everything that has happened in the course of my life, just by writing this book has help me gained a whole new perspective on life and gave me a true purpose on why I'm here on Earth. I'm dedicating this book to you so you can find your life purpose and share your testimony with the world so people can finally seek Christ for deliverance and salvation.

Till then, have a wonderful and blessed day. I pray that we finally meet in person and spread the gospel.

Your forever friend and brother in Christ,

Robert Smith

To My Loving Aunt Lila M. Pearson (R.I.P)

I truly want to take the time to personally thank you for being another big impact in my life. It's been hard to believe you're gone from this world. It almost feels as if you're still here and I can still hear your voice speaking to me. I want you to know that we all miss you and love you always.

ACKNOWLEDGEMENTS

With special thanks:

- To my mother **Janice**. Thank you for bringing me into this world. I want to thank you for everything you have done for me and knew me when others judged and persecuted me. Thank you for being there in my life and being my main support through it all.

- To **Della**. Thank you for being like another mother to me. I thank you for the love, guidance and wisdom that you showed to me each and every time we connect.

- To **Candace**. Thank you for being a sister that I've never had but always wanted. I appreciate your unconditional love for me and you always look out for me.

- To **Samarah, Jasmine, and Chris Jr**. I love you guys so much. Thank you for letting me be your favorite uncle ☺

- To my brother **LaDarrin**. I still love you even till this very day. Even though we may have our differences from time to time, we will always be blood brothers.

- To all my friends and to those that read this book. Thank you from the bottom of my heart. I appreciate you being there for me and supporting me 100% all the way with this. I pray that this book resonate with you and touches your heart as well as others to not only help motivate you to become very successful in your divine purpose, but to guide you through the trials of this life.

TABLE OF CONTENT

Chapter 1:
The Plan, Vision, and the Purpose

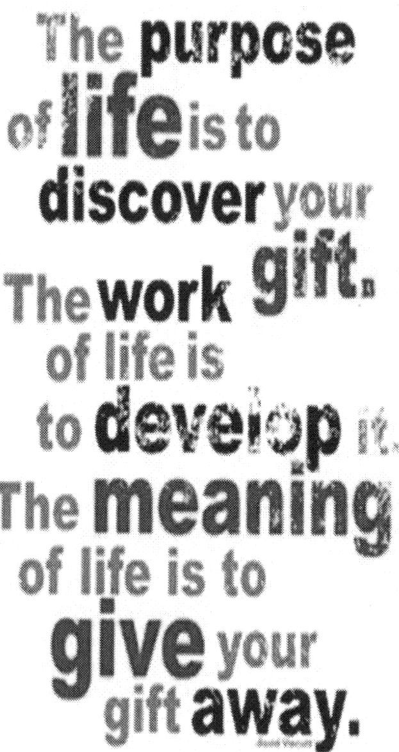

It All Begins With A Spoken Word

I wanted to personally take the time to reflect on things. Have you ever sat back and looked at everything around us and wondered how did everything come into its very existence? Everything in this life that exist all came first from a spoken word. Someone had the idea to create it and spoke it as an affirmation followed up with action. As a matter of fact, this world that we are living in began as a thought and a spoken word from our Lord.

Psalm 33:9 (KJV)

9 For he spake, and it was done; he commanded, and it stood fast.

Hebrews 11:3 (KJV)

3 Through faith we understand that the worlds were framed by the word of God, so that things which are seen were not made of things which do appear.

We also see evidence of it in ***Genesis 1:1-31***

Genesis 1:1-31 (KJV)

1 In the beginning God created the heaven and the earth.

2 And the earth was without form, and void; and darkness was upon the face of the deep. And the Spirit of God moved upon the face of the waters.

3 And God said, Let there be light: and there was light.

4 And God saw the light, that it was good: and God divided the light from the darkness.

5 And God called the light Day, and the darkness he called Night. And the evening and the morning were the first day.

6 And God said, Let there be a firmament in the midst of the waters, and let it divide the waters from the waters.

7 And God made the firmament, and divided the waters which were under the firmament from the waters which were above the firmament: and it was so.

8 And God called the firmament Heaven. And the evening and the morning were the second day.

9 And God said, Let the waters under the heaven be gathered together unto one place, and let the dry land appear: and it was so.

10 And God called the dry land Earth; and the
gathering together of the waters called he Seas: and
God saw that it was good.

11 And God said, Let the earth bring forth grass, the
herb yielding seed, and the fruit tree yielding fruit
after his kind, whose seed is in itself, upon the earth:
and it was so.

12 And the earth brought forth grass, and herb yielding
seed after his kind, and the tree yielding fruit, whose
seed was in itself, after his kind: and God saw that it
was good.

13 And the evening and the morning were the third
day.

14 And God said, Let there be lights in the firmament
of the heaven to divide the day from the night; and let
them be for signs, and for seasons, and for days, and
years:

15 And let them be for lights in the firmament of the
heaven to give light upon the earth: and it was so.

16 And God made two great lights; the greater light to
rule the day, and the lesser light to rule the night: he
made the stars also.

17 And God set them in the firmament of the heaven to
give light upon the earth,

18 And to rule over the day and over the night, and to
divide the light from the darkness: and God saw that it
was good.

19 And the evening and the morning were the fourth
day.

20 And God said, Let the waters bring forth abundantly
the moving creature that hath life, and fowl that may
fly above the earth in the open firmament of heaven.

21 And God created great whales, and every living
creature that moveth, which the waters brought forth
abundantly, after their kind, and every winged fowl
after his kind: and God saw that it was good.

22 And God blessed them, saying, Be fruitful, and
multiply, and fill the waters in the seas, and let fowl
multiply in the earth.

23 And the evening and the morning were the fifth day.

24 And God said, Let the earth bring forth the living
creature after his kind, cattle, and creeping thing, and
beast of the earth after his kind: and it was so.

25 And God made the beast of the earth after his kind,
and cattle after their kind, and every thing that
creepeth upon the earth after his kind: and God saw
that it was good.

26 And God said, Let us make man in our image, after
our likeness: and let them have dominion over the fish
of the sea, and over the fowl of the air, and over the
cattle, and over all the earth, and over every creeping
thing that creepeth upon the earth.

27 So God created man in his own image, in the image
of God created he him; male and female created he
them.

28 And God blessed them, and God said unto them, Be fruitful, and multiply, and replenish the earth, and subdue it: and have dominion over the fish of the sea, and over the fowl of the air, and over every living thing that moveth upon the earth.

29 And God said, Behold, I have given you every herb bearing seed, which is upon the face of all the earth, and every tree, in the which is the fruit of a tree yielding seed; to you it shall be for meat.

30 And to every beast of the earth, and to every fowl of the air, and to every thing that creepeth upon the earth, wherein there is life, I have given every green herb for meat: and it was so.

31 And God saw every thing that he had made, and, behold, it was very good. And the evening and the morning were the sixth day.

Before God created the universe and the world, He already had the vision and saw the purpose of creating it. He created all the things with the end in mind.

What's My Purpose in Life?

I know that you've probably came to a point in your life where you began to ask yourself these questions....

- *"Why am I even here?"*
- *"What's my purpose here on Earth?"*
- *"What else lies ahead of me?"*

I have newsflash for you, you're not the only who have asked those questions. In fact, these questions have become "The Million Dollar" question to most people. The reason why these questions have become very difficult for us to answer is because we gotten to a place that we've became so busy with everything else in this life (My acronym for the word **"BUSY"** means **Being Under Satan's Yoke**) such as our careers, school, family life, social life, and all other things that we've completely lost all sight and focus on God and His will for our lives. Most of us are not even following the path that God paved for all of us to go on. We're so caught up into everything else that we've never got a real chance to sit down to think for ourselves what we truly want out of this life. Sadly, most people ultimately go to the grave with dreams that never came into fulfillment. There is an old saying that goes like this, "The richest place on Earth isn't some exotic city, some fabulous island, or some tropical beach; it's the graveyard. In graveyards are filled with dead bodies full of treasure "dreams" that never was born or ever took root. Those dreams or "treasures" could have been businesses, books, inventions, film, television series, CD's, buildings, institutions, or other ideas that could benefit mankind. Because they allowed fear to enter their spirit, they took all that to the grave with them.

The great news is that we can break that yoke right this instant. We all have the power to change what is going on in our lives. The real "truth" is that you have complete power and authority to chart the course. In fact, God wants all of us to experience real love, real joy, real peace, happiness, fulfillment, and a divine purpose. All of these things are possible and is right at our fingertips. This happens only when we constantly seek out and build a relationship with Him. This is what the Bible says about this topic……

Matthew 6:33 (KJV)

But seek ye first the kingdom of God, and his righteousness; and all these things shall be added unto you.

Jeremiah 29:11-13 (KJV)

11 For I know the thoughts that I think toward you, saith the LORD, thoughts of peace, and not of evil, to give you an expected end.

12 Then shall ye call upon me, and ye shall go and pray unto me, and I will hearken unto you.

13 And ye shall seek me, and find me, when ye shall search for me with all your heart.

As you can see the Bible makes this very clear. If you really want to experience God's best, you have to pray and seek Him out.

Having the Vision

When I was younger, I saw myself being very successful in life. I would imagine myself traveling around the globe, speaking to lots of people, and sharing my story. I also saw myself having a very beautiful wife and two to three kids by my side. I could just see myself being happy and joyful seeing that I'm living my dream life. I had this dream of the perfect life ever since I was six years old.

I was unaware of the circumstances or lifestyle during that time of my life. I have to say this, when you're a child, imagination was everything. I guess you can say that I'm a dreamer. The thing about having a dream is that when you have an action plan behind that dream, it's no longer a dream anymore. That dream has become a goal.

Did I know exactly how that dream was going to happen? No I didn't. As a matter of fact, I didn't even have the slightest clue how it was going to happen. I kept saying that in due time the idea will come to me. I will eventually attract the way. I want you to think about this for a moment. Did you know how you were going to be formed, how you would look, or how you would show up here on Earth? The answer is no. You were no more than a pure thought floating out in space. God made it possible for two people; a man and a woman to procreate and nine months later you showed up. In other words, you were a mere thought that was conceived by two people that had vision of having a family and that thought manifested into a physical equivalent.

The perfect example of having vision would be Jeremiah from the Bible. According to the Word of God, Jeremiah was called to be a prophet to Israel. God even declared that even before Jeremiah was conceived he was known by God and was set apart for His divine purpose. The walk that Jeremiah would take in his life was not going to be easy. As a matter of fact, Jeremiah was best known for the prophet who endured. He served as God's faithful messenger despite many attempts on his life. Before Jeremiah began his chosen journey, he told God that he couldn't speak because he was too young. At that time of his life he was believed to be around 18-20 years old ***(Jeremiah 1:6)***. God answered back in ***(Jeremiah 1:7)*** telling him do not let his age be a hindrance to him. Then He instructed Jeremiah to not let the people intimidate him as he goes forth and deliver God's message.

Jeremiah finally gave in and followed God's instructions. Jeremiah developed the courage and stamina to prophesize destruction to the kings, princes, priests, and the people of Judah. Jeremiah was clearly telling them that if they did not give up their sinful ways, repent, and turn to follow God they would certainly face capture, death, or so much worst punishment. Do you really think that they actually listened? No, in fact they kept living and indulging in sin. The people of Israel turned away from God, like a married spouse who commits adultery, disregarding the covenant they agreed to after coming out of Egypt ***(Exodus 24:3)***.

Before I get into this a bit further, let's break down the importance of a covenant and what it is. A covenant is defined as a promise to engage in or refrain from a specific action. I'm going to use this for an example.

When you get married or at least have walked down the aisle to say your vows to each other, you're verbally signing an agreement to God and one another that you will be completely faithful. You agreed to support one another and stick it out regardless of what life brings into the marriage. Same rules apply to you when you devote yourself to God when you repent of your ways and follow Jesus Christ.

Unfortunately, these promises get broken every single day. When a person breaks their commitment especially in their marriage, they're allowing all types of attacks to enter in their marriage. These attacks could be numerous of things like the mistress may end up getting pregnant from the affair, the passing of STDs to the other spouse, or both the cheater and the other person get caught and their "affair" is now being revealed to the unexpected spouse. These problems can really put your marriage in serious trouble.

Same thing applies when a person breaks their commitment and a classic example of this would be when person gets saved. When a person gets delivered, they make a verbal covenant or "agreement" that you will never turn back to their "old ways" or live a sinful life. Once the person commit a sin or keep doing it; not only they're opening up themselves to any disaster to come into their life, but they're bringing judgment on themselves before the Lord.

- BACK TO JEREMIAH'S STORY…

Let's get back to the part about Jeremiah. When the people of Israel broke their covenant, God was very disappointed with the nation and had no choice but carry out justice. However, God was very compassionate towards Jeremiah and wanted to protect him during his darkest hour. God advises Jeremiah not to marry because He didn't want to see his wife and children suffer miserably ***(Jeremiah 16:2-4)***.

Jeremiah's ultimate vision was to see the people of Judah and Israel to completely turn away from their sins and wrong doing and turn to God. This is what God really wanted all along for mankind.

Chapter 2:
My Early Life Growing Up

Growing Pains

I have to say that through most of my life it's been a struggle. I was born on June 22, 1983 on a Wednesday afternoon. My birthplace is High Point, NC. I grew up on Southside. I have two other siblings; one full brother and one half-brother on my dad's side.

During the early days of my life, I've seen and experienced many things. There were good moments as well as trials and tribulations especially growing up in the inner city.

During the time when I was younger and both my parents were still together, I can remember way back when they would have cookouts on the weekends and invite family and friends over. They would be kickin' back while having steaks, chicken, hamburgers on the grill while listening to some "Old School" classics. They would listen to music from The O'Jay's, Betty White, Gladys Knight, The Commodores, and the list would go on and on. This is where I got my 'Old School" roots from sort of speak.

I would sit back and reminisce about the "old days" and I recalled my mother telling me about some of the things I've done when I was a child. When I was very young, I went to Emmanuel Baptist Church in Thomasville, NC. The preacher at that time was Rev. McLendon. During the time of the service, they started collecting the tithes and offering. As everyone was standing up and getting ready to give their offerings, my cousin grabbed me and put me in her arms as we're getting ready to give money as well. As we made our way to the altar to place our money in the offering plate, I swiped the offering plate and hid it behind my cousin's back as we're making our way back to our seats. No one even noticed that the collection plate was gone until someone seen the table with nothing to place the money in. The deacons and members of the church were scrambling around looking for the collection plate. Some of them were even wondering how the plate got gone so fast. About 20 minutes later, someone spotted the collection plate and said, "The baby got it, the baby got it." My cousin was in shocked because she didn't even notice that I even took the plate. When the plate was finally returned back to the altar, one of the members said, "The baby knows what momma needs." Everyone started laughing even the pastor. I guess this was a sign from the very beginning letting people know that I was going to take care of my mother. It makes me laugh every time I think about it.

A Home without a Support Beam

As I gotten a little bit older, I started seeing many changes around me. I got to see hardships especially in the home. My mom and dad were heading straight into a divorce which was very frustrating especially as a kid. I would see my dad leave and not coming back for days. Before I get into my story here, I am going to breakdown the meaning of being a father and a man from the Bible standpoint. Your age and what you possess doesn't make you a man. I want you to read a quote stated by Winston Churchill. He stated, "A man does what he must in spite of personal consequences, in spite of obstacles and dangers and pressures and that is the basis of all human morality." When we look into the New Testament, the Bible makes it very clear on how a family is supposed to be. It also gives and defines the role for the husband and wife. Let's take a closer look at ***Ephesians 5***.

Ephesians 5:22-33 (KJV)

22 Wives, submit yourselves unto your own husbands, as unto the Lord.

23 For the husband is the head of the wife, even as Christ is the head of the church: and he is the saviour of the body.

24 Therefore as the church is subject unto Christ, so let the wives be to their own husbands in every thing.

25 Husbands, love your wives, even as Christ also loved the church, and gave himself for it;

26 That he might sanctify and cleanse it with the washing of water by the word,

27 That he might present it to himself a glorious church, not having spot, or wrinkle, or any such thing; but that it should be holy and without blemish.

28 So ought men to love their wives as their own bodies. He that loveth his wife loveth himself.

29 For no man ever yet hated his own flesh; but nourisheth and cherisheth it, even as the Lord the church:

30 For we are members of his body, of his flesh, and of his bones.

31 For this cause shall a man leave his father and mother, and shall be joined unto his wife, and they two shall be one flesh.

32 This is a great mystery: but I speak concerning Christ and the church.

33 Nevertheless let every one of you in particular so love his wife even as himself; and the wife see that she reverence her husband.

The Bible also emphasizes that men should also be a leader. Paul states in ***Colossians 1:25***, "Whereof I am made a minister, according to the dispensation of God which is given to me for you, to fulfill the word of God." Paul saw himself as a servant rather than just a professional in his field. Jesus Christ gave us an example of this attitude of being a leader. According to the Bible, here are scriptures that explain it to the exact "T."

John 13:3-5 (KJV)

3 Jesus knowing that the Father had given all things into his hands, and that he was come from God, and went to God;

4 He riseth from supper, and laid aside his garments; and took a towel, and girded himself.

5 After that he poureth water into a bason, and began to wash the disciples' feet, and to wipe them with the towel wherewith he was girded.

John 13:12-15 (KJV)

12 So after he had washed their feet, and had taken his garments, and was set down again, he said unto them, Know ye what I have done to you?

13 Ye call me Master and Lord: and ye say well; for so I am.

14 If I then, your Lord and Master, have washed your feet; ye also ought to wash one another's feet.

15 For I have given you an example, that ye should do as I have done to you.

Philippians 2:3-8 (KJV)

3 Let nothing be done through strife or vainglory; but in lowliness of mind let each esteem other better than themselves.

4 Look not every man on his own things, but every man also on the things of others.

5 Let this mind be in you, which was also in Christ Jesus:

6 Who, being in the form of God, thought it not robbery to be equal with God:

7 But made himself of no reputation, and took upon him the form of a servant, and was made in the likeness of men:

8 And being found in fashion as a man, he humbled himself, and became obedient unto death, even the death of the cross.

1 Peter 5:5-7 (KJV)

5 Likewise, ye younger, submit yourselves unto the elder. Yea, all of you be subject one to another, and be clothed with humility: for God resisteth the proud, and giveth grace to the humble.

6 Humble yourselves therefore under the mighty hand of God, that he may exalt you in due time:

7 Casting all your care upon him; for he careth for you.

John 3:30 (KJV)

30 He must increase, but I must decrease.

As we see mostly in the book of John, Jesus shows the disciples the nature of leadership God's way. As Jesus Christ began to take off his garment and humbled himself like a servant and wash the feet of the disciples, the disciples were beside themselves. This was not how a leader should behave. Jesus simply told them that He was giving them a model of the kind of leadership He desired. This kind of leadership is called "**servant leadership**." Just to give you a clear definition on this type of leadership, it's defined as being in position to "**serve others first**" rather than leading. I will touch on this subject more as we're going along through the course of this book.

Men are supposed to be the providers. The man should feel a great responsibility to provide for the family. The woman was created for the sole purpose to assist the man and maintaining support for the family. I'm going to give you this verse.

Genesis 2:18 (KJV)

18 And the Lord God said, It is not good that the man should be alone; I will make him an help meet for him.

Keep in mind that man is not only to provide financial support, but is called to provide emotional and physical support as well.

Men also are served as protectors. Let's take a closer look at this. The man is responsible for the physical security of his family. God designed men to have more strength than women and has also given men a desire to be protectors. This is very vital for the man to know this. To all the guys out there, you should use your God-given ability to protect your wife and family and ensure especially your wife that she feels secure. The love that you must show is the type of love that is mentioned in ***John 15:13***.

John 15:13 (KJV)

13 Greater love hath no man than this, that a man lay down his life for his friends.

Your woman must know that you will protect her even if it means putting your life on the line to save her.

I'm going to continue on with my story here. As I would see my own father gone for days, my mother is left all alone taking care of the household. We were too young at the time to process any of these events going on. I could tell that my mom was very saddened with what's going on. As time progressed on, my mother and father had separated and this really jeopardized the home. One of the biggest heartbreaks that I've encountered was when I was at school. During my fourth grade year we had an event called "Father & Son Day." Fathers would come to school to spend time with their kids. When it was time to go to lunch, I would see many of my classmate's fathers arrive at the school to see their kids during lunchtime. As the dads would come and sit down with their children, I noticed my dad coming in the cafeteria. I was really excited to see him because it was the very first time that I've seen my dad since the separation. We both looked at each other and he waved at me, but he began to walk in the other direction and sat down with who I later found out was his girlfriend's children. My world at that moment just crumbled. Could you imagine how disappointing I was to see my own father that helped gave me life in this world just turn away from me like that?

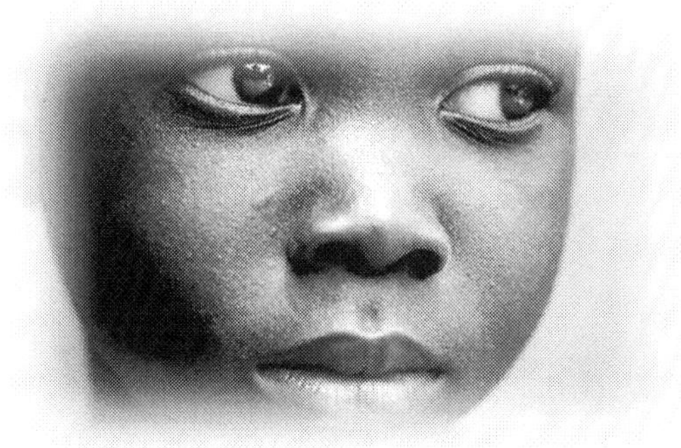

At that time, I felt devastated. All I would see is my classmates and other students with their dads and I'm the only person at my school without mines. I said this to myself many times this. When I get older and start having my own family, I will never treat my children the exact same way my own dad done me. I'm going to be the one to break this vicious cycle.

This is my take on what a father's role in the home should be. A father symbolizes a support beam to a house. In order for a house to stand tall and not sink, it should have two things; **a strong foundation** as well as a very **strong support beam**. If the foundation is weak and there is no support bean, then your home has a very strong chance of falling apart. This means if your relationship isn't built on the principles that God teaches in the Bible and the man neglects his responsibilities that he vowed to do, the woman will be in a position of struggling to manage everything in the home.

Being Misunderstood

When I was younger, I was diagnosed with Attention Deficit Disorder (ADD). For those that really don't quite understand what is Attention Deficit Disorder (ADD) is, this is the definition. It's basically a neurological disorder of the brain. It's where the brain doesn't produce enough dopamine which is responsible for the regulation of attention, impulse control and motor activity. The problems that those with Attention Deficit Disorder has are listed below

- Often does not give close attention to details or makes careless mistakes in schoolwork, work, or other activities.
- Often has trouble keeping attention on tasks or play activities
- Often does not seem to listen when spoken to directly.

- Often does not follow instructions and fails to finish schoolwork, chores, or duties in the workplace (not due to oppositional behavior or failure to understand instructions).

- Often have trouble organizing activities.

- Often avoids, dislikes, or doesn't want to do things that take a lot of mental effort for a long period (such as schoolwork or homework).

- Often loses things needed for tasks and activities (e.g. toys, school assignments, pencils, books, or tools).

- Is often easily distracted.

- Is often forgetful in daily activities.

ADD/ADHD Simplified

I want to simplify this even further for those that don't fully understand the disorder. Just imagine ADD/ADHD as a faulty television set. You can get all the channels from 01-125, but the most important channels that focus on planning, organization, sequence, and process are blocked out or basically put it "distorted." The only channels that are working are stations (brain signals) that focus strictly on entertainment (those that stimulates us). Another issue is that the television set (our brains) is constantly on auto-surf with no one controlling the remote. This means that we constantly jump from one task to another without even fully completing or seeing our original task all the way through. With everything coming at us so rapidly, we struggle with slowing things down because our brain is working too fast.

During the time that I was young, I had ear surgery as well. Tubes were placed in both ears to correct my hearing problem. One of the tubes fell in my right ear, which punctured a hole there. This makes it very difficult for me to hear anything on my right side. Only a very few people actually know what's going on with me. Just with these medical problems I had going on with me had literally turned my life upside down. I was ridiculed constantly by neighborhood kids, teachers, and even adults of being "mentally retarded or slow." All these things happened to me right around 7 years old and the sad part is that I still face this issue till this day. I can remember many times I would come home in tears because of the harassment and torment I would get from school alone then the neighborhood. This had leaded me to get into fights at school as well as in the neighborhood. When I did get into trouble at school, I was getting the label as being a "bad and disruptive student" by teachers and principals. That wasn't even the case at all. I was just fed up with all the verbal abuse and torment from people and the only way I could react is to simply defend myself.

My Dating Life Back In the Early Days

Love can be a very beautiful thing to experience especially in the good old days of high school. I was attending school in High Point, NC at this time. When I was there, my hope was to hook up the most popular girl in school. I thought that just by "hooking up" with the most popular girl in school would give me that boost of confidence that I needed. I quickly realized that it wasn't the case at all. Back then, I was treated even worst by girls especially "African-American girls." Back then, many of them founded me to be "unattractive" and that I was "slow." It almost felt like I never fit in anywhere I go even when it came down to having a relationship. At this point in my life as a youth, I didn't think my life was worth living anymore because I saw it as this; If my life is going this bad now, I can only imagine how it's going to be down the road and I was ready to give up. I was really going through a major depression and about to kill myself. I later got the help needed to get me through this pain that I was enduring in my life. I ended up transferring from the school in High Point, NC to a school in Jamestown, NC.

After I started going there, things did turn around for me. I was still getting teased a lot, but some amazing things did happen for me. I did found love, well so I thought. During that time, I was a senior in high school and the girl I was dating back then was a sophomore. I can remember the date, which was February 17, 2001. We met in the school cafeteria were her friend approached me and gave me her number on a sticky note. We began to get to know each other a couple of days afterwards. After school, I would take her home and it almost seems like time stood still. I didn't want it to end. After one day of dropping her home from school, I had my first kiss which felt amazing especially from a person that never had any luck with the ladies.

We dated hot and heavy during my high school year. We were voted "Couple of the Year." Most of our classmates even thought that we were going to get married after high school. Several months later the relationship took a nosedive and came to an abrupt end. It was a very heartbreaking moment especially to me. It actually took me longer to get over it being that it was my very first relationship I ever had. I had to realize that there will be better opportunities that will come along the way as life goes on.

As time goes on by, I did meet and been in other relationships. I still had gotten the same treatment as before. When I begin a relationship, it would go really well at first. When time progresses on, the women I was dating would turn against me. All I would face is lots of criticism especially when it was coming from "African-American" women. None of the women would actually take the time to actually know what's going on with me. Instead they would put me down and plainly give up on me. After all the failed attempts, I decided to just focus my efforts on other things and left the dating scene for a while.

Future
Present
Past

Chapter 3:
Facing the Real World

Surviving In the Corporate American World

By this time of my life, I was fresh out of high school and was trying to make it on my own in the world of corporate America. Being that I was diagnosed with Attention Deficit Disorder (ADD), it was a very difficult challenge for me. I was truly trying my very best to manage it and fit in sort of speak. As I was making several attempts to adjust in the corporate America world, I was finding it very difficult to fit in. Every job that I've gotten even from the time I was 15 years old, I would get cold stares and sometimes even mocked at. When I got into trouble on the job or was messing up quite a lot, I would be approached and told by many supervisors that "I'm too slow" or "I can't comprehend what's going on or being given to me." During all of this, I was trying really hard to hide my ADD/ADHD. I would see the frustration on their faces when it came to dealing with me. I would play it off and tell them "I'm sorry; I'm just very forgetful sometimes." There have been many times I would get distracted and when things got worse, I would end up getting fired.

This pattern would happen over and over each year. After looking at everything then and evaluating things a bit, I came to the conclusion that having ADD/ADHD was hindering me in the corporate American world. I began questioning myself whether or not I even had a chance in life period.

Trying To Find Peace in a Very Dark Place

My days living in High Point, NC have been nothing but traumatizing to me. Being in a town like that and experiencing these kinds of tragedies, one must stay prayed up. My mother was the perfect example of perseverance. When times gotten tough and I mean really tough, she held on to her faith and always stayed strong because she knew in her heart that the hardships and the struggle that we've faced growing up will be finally over one day. Through my mom, she helped build my faith and trust in the Lord as well as the Bible. During that time in my life I was going through a lot and was looking for guidance and direction. We began looking for a real church or at least a church that we could call home. In our hometown of High Point, NC there are many churches around. Some of the churches that we've went to were great, but I really couldn't get into what they teach or it just didn't move me in a way to keep me coming back. After a year or so searching, a friend of the family came to our home and told us about a church in Archdale, NC that we should visit. We were very hesitant about going, but decided to take a leap of faith and visit the place anyway. At that particular time, the church that we've visited had a small group of members attending. One thing that I did admire about the church was the messages that were being delivered during the time. I kept going back and back for about a year before I decided to join the church. During this point in my life, I thought I really found a church home.

Still Trapped In the Maze

During the time of joining the church, I was just getting settled and adjusted to everything. Still at that moment things wasn't working out. Nothing was opening up for me as far as job opportunities goes. All I would do is work odd jobs here and there. Being in a small town, the chances of finding anything was very slim. I could recall a time when I went to the employment office and a few people even told not only me but several people not to even look for anything in High Point, NC. While I was trying to figure things out, my family came down from Peekskill, NY to visit us. While my family relatives were in town, I decided to ask my cousin what he did for a living. He began to tell me that he started his own business removing asbestos from residential homes and commercial buildings in New York. I was intrigued by the idea and thought this might be something to look into so I began to plan my trip going to New York for the summer.

$10 Bucks and a Dream

I've always said that when you want something bad enough, you will do anything in your power to get it or achieve it no matter the circumstances. My wish was to leave my hometown of High Point, North Carolina and never returning back to it. My next wish was to start my own business to be able to support myself and my family. I knew in my heart that I will never be happy living in High Point, NC. Even things at church weren't going right at all. I started to notice how members at church were acting towards me. Most of them were looking down at me and thought I was lazy, incompetent, and didn't want to do anything with my life which was never the case. I was even being compared to other people. To me that's like comparing apples to oranges. I kept getting this vibe and I gotten to the point that I wanted out. My mother saw what was going on and decided to help me purchase my ticket to see my family in New York. I was really excited about going to New York being that I can explore my options and get to know the place. I love the feeling of stepping out and exploring new places. The one thing that I didn't have was extra money on me to do anything else.

I ended up pawning all my DVD's and only got $10 bucks for all of them. I was quite disappointed, but if this is all I could get then so be it. My mindset then was that no matter what, I was going to make it out of this hellish place and become something in life.

Chapter 4:
Welcome to New York

My Arrival to New York

Right before I was about to head out to New York, I did get some love from many friends and a few family members. Of course some people that knew I was leaving from the neighborhood were saying, "You'll be right back here." I was doing my very best to tune all that negativity out and just focus on making opportunities happen for me in New York. I was so excited about leaving North Carolina that nothing was going to neither stop me nor bring me down. I had my bags packed and my bus ticket in my hand ready for this move. My mother gave me a hug and was saying to me that she wishes me the best as well as a safe trip to New York. After we gave each other hugs, my ride came ready to take me to the bust station.

I board the bus moments after it arrived over 45 minutes later. I knew from the beginning that this was going to be a long bus ride going to New York, a 12 hour long bus ride to be exact. Once I've arrived at the Port Authority in New York, that's when my whole world changed.

I had arrived in New York around 12:45am Thursday morning and people where out and about just like if it was 12 o'clock in the afternoon. That's when I realized why people call New York City, "The city that never sleeps." To me, New York was the "Hustle State" mainly because people grind 24/7. All I would see is limos, taxis, Hummers, tricked out BMWs going by and of course New York finest "THE NYPD." I say within 45 minutes later, my cousin picks me up from the station taking me to my aunt's apartment in Peekskill, NY. When I got to my aunt's apartment which was around 1:45am early Friday morning, I just crashed on the rollout couch and got some much needed sleep.

Getting a Taste of 'The Big Apple"

Morning arrived and I woke up to a very hot meal. I remembered having 3 fluffy pancakes, eggs, ham & bacon, and to top that off; a huge "Red Apple" which I found out was symbolic. The apple meant this, "Welcome to the Big Apple" which started to be a tradition in our family. About an hour later, my cousin came by to take me on his job. My cousin in New York owns and operates his own asbestos removal and demolishing company. What my cousin does is go into homes or commercial buildings and perform inspection. He inspect for asbestos, mold, or anything that could cause health related problems to individuals. After he checks and discovers the problem, he would either hire a crew of people or would go solo to remove whatever he finds that's harmful. When I was with him, we would go to different locations within Peekskill as well as outside of the city. I could recall a time when he took me to one of the homes that was being renovated. He had to do an inspection there, but I have to say that house that he had to do an inspection at was huge. The home was estimated around 1.2 million I believe and it kind of reminded me of the home from the T.V. show Fresh Prince of Bel-Air.

After the day had ended, he took me back to my aunt's apartment to wind down for a bit. Later on that evening, he came back to take me out of the town. We went out to Manhattan to cruise the strip for a bit. I saw some awesome things when I was there. He showed me some of the hottest nightclubs, shops, and restaurants in Manhattan, NY. He took me to a great Jamaican soul food restaurant in downtown Manhattan. I thought this was exciting because I never had tried any Jamaican food before. I had ordered the Teriyaki Chicken with jambalaya red beans and rice, collard greens, fried cornbread, and lemonade. I have to say that the way they prepared it was the best food I've ever eaten. Afterwards, we decided to explore more of the city one more time before calling it a night.

My Big "Birthday" Surprise

I had just turned 21 around that time and had mentioned my birthday to my folks when I was talking with them over the phone before leaving to New York. When I was there, everything seemed to be going great. The 4th of July was fast approaching and my cousins there was helping me make money anyway I possibly can. I still had that $10 bucks in my pocket and I told them, "Yes ma'am….I gotta make that cash." One of my cousin's works at a veteran's hospital in Peekskill but she also make side money scrapping metal and aluminum cans. When she got off work she would come get me and take me out to places that would save her bags and sometimes boxes of aluminum cans. I would do pick-ups and load them in the back of her jeep to take them back to her home. We would do this for about a week and once we had all that we could handle, we would take them to one of the recycling centers in the city to cash them out. Their recycling centers operated similar to "Coin-Star" that you would see in stores like Food Lion, but instead of inserting pennies, nickels, and dimes in the machine to get a voucher to get cash back; you're inserting cans, plastic, and glass bottles in the machine to get a voucher to get cash. I remembered using it and ended up cashed out with $67.00. I gave the money to my cousin but instead, she just told me to keep the money and any more pick-ups we did from the time of the 4th is your money. As the week reached its end and we did have more pick-ups to make, I winded up with $100.00 in my pocket. I started looking back and said this, "Man! I came all this way from North Carolina with only $10 bucks to my name and made $100.00 without even a J.O.B. (Just Over Broke) and manage to make money on my own with the help of my cousin." She told me this phrase that I'll never forget.

"To Get What You Want In This Life….You Got To Hustle For It"

~Annie Tatum (My Cousin)

I got to say that my cousin Annie was my best teacher when it came to "The School of Hustling." She used to make me laugh when I was around her, but she spoke the real truth when it came to "making money." The 4th came and I just founded out that my cousin's friend was having a huge block party. My aunt and cousins bought me an outfit and I was looking all fresh and clean. Like "Outkast" said in one of their songs, "So fresh and So Clean…Clean." So anyway, we made our way to the party and it was slam packed. There were so many cars packed everywhere that we had to park three blocks down at an abandoned store in the neighborhood. Everything was great from the music, the food, the folks, and just the way it was all put together. We didn't leave till 10pm that night. My cousin Annie had me collecting all the cans and bottles and there were a lot of them. Luckily the bins that people were putting the cans and bottles in were labeled, so this made it a lot easy on us. All I had to do is grab the whole bag and tie them up and take them to the car. We took them to one of the recycling centers that following afternoon and gotten $75.00. Now I had $175.00 in my pocket and when my cousin dropped me off, she told me to be ready next week because I'm going to somewhere special. That whole week I'm trying to guess what was it I was going to. She took that following Friday off work and come early around 9:30am to come get me. With my cousin Annie was also my other cousin Lillie that was riding with her. I was all dressed and ready to leave out. She told me on the way going that we were going to Connecticut. I didn't know why we were going but it didn't matter. By the time we approached the place I soon realized where I was at and were like, "Oh My."

I've always wanted to go to a casino for my birthday but had no idea that my cousins had this planned out for me. When we got inside the place, they told me "Happy Belated Birthday" from us cuzzo!" I got to tell you guys, I had a ball there. I had the money saved up and was ready to have fun. I dropped $40 playing the slots and made my money right back plus some extra. After 2 hours of playing I had over $300.00 more than what I came in with. I had around $375.00 and I just decided to walk away. I said this, "If I came in to this place and made more than what I had from the beginning, then it's time to play it safe and walk away." Unfortunately, my cousins didn't do the same. They made a lot of money but lost it all too. Like the saying goes, "The house always wins." After spending the entire day at the casino, we decided to head back. I ended up driving back to New York. Let's just say it was an experience to say the least.

The Sun Finally Sets For Me in New York

I can truly say that I had a blast staying in New York. I've gotten the chance to meet some great people as well as sightseeing. I've also gotten the privilege to see things that I never would have thought imagined while I was with my cousins. I've also got to visit Mount Olivet Baptist Church which was my aunt's church located in Peekskill, NY.

(Mount Olivet Baptist Church Peekskill, NY)

I used to go to this church with my aunt Lila Pearson every Sunday when I was in New York. I can recall many great memories there while attending the church. I really enjoyed listening to the sermons from the pastor that was preaching there at the time back around 2005. After many weeks went on by, it was time for me to head back to North Carolina. I've dreaded going back to that place and wanted to avoid that place as much as possible. I didn't want to go to a place where all I got was "mean mugs & cold stares" which is a quote from Tupac's song "Death around the Corner." I didn't even want to see that place. No matter how much hatred I've felt towards my hometown and state, I had to return back.

Back in High Point, NC

When I've arrived back to High Point, NC which I really dreaded the most, I didn't even get a great welcome back. All I kept getting was a lot of questions being asked by some of the people that knew I left and especially church members. The questions that I would mostly get asked was, "Why did I come back here? I though you left for good." When I begin to tell them why, I started getting negative responses back. Those responses would be like, "I told you so" or "I knew it wouldn't work out." At this point, I really started to question their whole mindset. I'm thinking to myself, "How could anyone of you guys say and preach about having faith and having Jesus Christ in your life, but can say the most disrespectful things towards anyone that's trying to improve their life?" Then I quickly realize the type of people I was dealing with.

Betrayal by the Church

Now before I begin to tell my story, I'm going to "drop some serious knowledge" on how Satan works. Satan's whole agenda is to deceive humanity. The sole purpose of why he wants to do this is to get us to believe into an idea or thought that isn't true. If you're a believer who is totally ignorant of the Word of God, you are more likely to be deceived and accept Satan's lies as real truth. After this seed has been sown in the head, the devil starts to put this stronghold in your mind. If you truly want to know what the true definition of a mental stronghold is, it's this.....

A **mental stronghold** is an incorrect thinking pattern based upon errors and lies that a believer has accepted as truth.

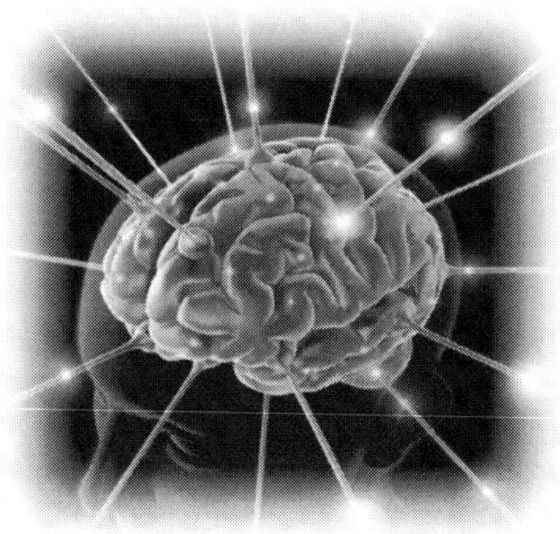

I'm going to continue here with my story and then break everything down for you on how much these lies had made a negative impact on my life.

When I went back to my church in High Point, everything from that moment changed. I noticed that I was being treated unfairly. I would be shunned and ignored. It almost felt like I wasn't even wanted there at all or anywhere for that matter. On one particular Sunday evening, the church held an afternoon service, but the message that was being preached was mostly geared towards the women. The message that was being delivered to the congregation was something that went along the guidelines of "Finding Love." The woman that was speaking was an older woman somewhere around in her early 40's around that time. As I recall, she was talking about how her and her now husband met. After she went on describing the entire relationship from how the union started to how they ended up married, she told all the men in the church that was single to never lose hope and that God will send the right person in their life. Afterwards, she had all the single men to come to the front of the church towards the pulpit. When all the men, including myself at that time came up to the pulpit, she began to speak to each and every one of us. As she continued to speak to us, one of the women stood up and said, "Nobody wants them. They're too slow." Being that I've heard this so many times in my life, that was insulting plus I was totally shocked at the same time. The reason that

I was totally blown away with the remark because of all the places that anyone could say such a horrible thing; it had to be said inside of a church. After the service I just felt like a sense of hopelessness because I'm in a city where nothing ever went right for me and all I kept getting was disappointments and being tormented just because nobody didn't even understood me at all. As time went on, there was something that was finally coming to the light about that church that I didn't know was going on. The pastor at that church announced that she was having an early Morning Prayer service in which all the members would come around 5am. That following week, some of the church members including me, my mother, and my brother came to the early Morning Prayer service. At the end of the entire service, the pastor went around to each member and confessing her wrong doings in which I thought was very odd. As she continued to go to everyone in the church, she then approached me. This pastor confessed to me that she was laughing behind my back and saying vulgar remarks about me and one of those remarks was calling me "slow."

That following week later, I went up to the front of the entire church and let everyone know how I felt about the negative remarks that was said about me and the treatment I was getting there. Soon afterwards, I left that church and never went back there again.

I went to another church in High Point, NC and at first things went well. I stayed at that church for a couple of years and I did become a deacon there. Things were going really great for me, well at least so it seems to be. I also dated one of the members there who was also a minister. I truly had thought everything was going to be ok. I had a really great job at a pharmaceutical company in High Point, NC, nice car which was a 2007 PT Cruiser, money in the bank, dressing in nice outfits and suits, and a woman in my life, and so much more.

I was so happy that things were going well for me that I literally thought that this was going to be my life. Then all of a sudden, it was all taken away from me. In 2008, I was wrongfully terminated from a job as an inspector at a pharmaceutical company right at the beginning of the New Year. I was denied my unemployment benefits in the beginning, and then later won my case two months later. When I got my unemployment benefits, of course it was half of what I was making. My money was gone within a year. As time went on, I began to lose everything I ever owned or anything that had my name on it. My car was repossessed, and my driver's license was being revoked. During that time, I've gotten into a lot of trouble with the law which lead to my arrest. I contacted my girlfriend to help bail me out of jail with the money that I had in my bank account. I was going to tell her how to gain access to it; but she denied my request and never even came to my aide. As a matter of fact, I confronted her about her actions and demanded to know why she didn't even help me. I reminded her of the times that I helped her in her time of need. When I needed help, I never get it. All I get in return is the "bad end" of the deal and disrespected for all my troubles. Her response was this, "I would have helped you. If you were in those "orange jump suits" picking up trash on the side of the road, I would have thrown trash out the window for you." All of this was coming from someone who supposed to have "Love Me." When I was in jail, I shared a cell with two other fellow inmates. One of the inmates looked at me and said this, "You don't belong here. You don't seem like the type of person that would do anything wrong. All the other inmates saw that right through you. You're a good hearted person that just got caught up and was at the wrong place at the wrong time."

I remember thinking this when I was looking out of the window of The Guilford County Correctional Facility, "God, please get me out of this place. I don't ever want to be in High Point, North Carolina anymore. Also give to me a woman that will never leave my side ever or turn against me. I deserve a much better life than what is being brought to me this very instant."

Later on that evening, my mother bailed me out of jail. She had a classmate that happens to be a bail bondman. When I got bailed out, I met my mother, my brother, and the bail bondman in the front office. I can say through all of this, Jesus Christ, my mother, and brother was there for me. I was so completely fed up with everything that I was facing in High Point, NC and the unfair treatment that I was getting from people especially the women I've dated there that I told my mother this, "With everything that's been going on with me in the city of High Point, it's time to finally leave this horrible place for good."

I was so ready to leave High Point, NC that I had U-Haul on speed dial. When I had around $1,500 in my bank account, I immediately got in touch with U-Haul and asked for the biggest truck they had. When I went to the place, I noticed that I wasn't the only one that wanted out of High Point, NC. There was a lady that came into the place and even told the store clerk that she's leaving High Point and was in need of a truck immediately. The store clerk was shocked, but knew exactly how it was living in High Point and the mentality of some of the people there simply because he lived there. I can even recall a time when I went to the store just to get packaging tape and moving boxes. The store clerk asked me, "Why so many boxes?" I simply told her that I was moving. The she asked me, "Are you moving to another area?" I responded by telling her this, "No. I'm moving completely out of the county and city all together." The lady shook my hand and was saying over and over this, "AMEN."

Amen!

REPEAT AFTER ME:
I AM FREE

Chapter 5:
The Big Move

The Great Escape

For the first time in a long time, I couldn't have been happier. I was finally leaving a place that literally gave me nothing but nightmares, frustration and disappointments. During that time, we've already found a great apartment in Burlington, NC that was affordable. We spent the past 2 weeks getting everything together for the move. Once we finally gotten everything in order, we were on our way on the highway to finally leave High Point, NC. From my perspective, the best view that I got to see High Point was seeing it in the rear view glass going 70 mph.

Life in Burlington, NC

When I got to the city of Burlington, I have to say that in the beginning everything was going ok. I was just settling in and getting to know the place better. I can say that compared to my hometown of High Point, Burlington is about the same. The only difference is that Burlington doesn't have a bus system which means that people that don't have a car is literally in trouble. On the flip side, I didn't know anyone so it kind of worked in my favor sort of speak. When I first moved here, I did try to find work in Burlington only to be disappointed. During that time in 2010, the jobs were scares. If anyone wanted to find work, you had to go out of the city. At that time I didn't have transportation of my own. As months went on by, it was getting tougher and tougher and at times, it almost felt like I was being tested on all levels. The only person that was working in the household was my mother. She was working in High Point still and would spend the week there at friend's homes and would come to Burlington on the weekend. She mostly kept the household up for a while until the only car that we had broken completely down.

"Being Tested"

I had learned this concept through life experiences. With each obstacle that comes our way only tests our faith.

LIFE HAS MANY
WAYS OF TESTING
A PERSON'S WILL,
EITHER BY HAVING
NOTHING HAPPEN AT
ALL OR BY HAVING
EVERYTHING HAPPEN
ALL AT ONCE

- PAULO COELHO -

With my mother's car now out of commission, everything in our life had started a domino effect. My mother couldn't go back to High Point to continue working so as a result of that, she lost her job. I was still trying to find work but was running into serious problems. One of the issues that I was facing at the time was my employment status. Being that I was out of work for so long, I was always looked over.

Another issue was that when I would go to job interviews, I would dress the part and everything I've done was right on point; I would still get ignored because people would still view me as "being slow" which bothered me a lot simply because I wasn't even given a real chance. I would get denied before I was even was given a real chance. As time went on, bills were going past due and we also would get late notices on the rent. I would have to hustle just to make ends meet and we stuck it out for as long as we could. Even with little odd jobs that I would do just to make it wasn't enough. We eventually lost our apartment and ended up staying with my brother.

During the time we stayed with my brother, we were still trying to do whatever we could to make it. My brother was working as a Certified Nursing Assistant at one of the nursing homes in Graham, NC. We had applied for jobs constantly, but still no luck finding anything. I was still hustling and doing whatever possible to make money. I remembered many times where I just would say to myself, "Did I make a terrible mistake moving here?" I had many people who knew our situation had told us that we should have done better research about Burlington before we moved there. I would answer back and say this, "I know in my heart that God won't bring me all this way just to leave us here down and without anything."

If God brings you to it,
He will bring you through it.

When I started thinking about the trials that I was facing and needed strength to get me through that moment, this scripture came to my mind.

Mark 4:35-41 (KJV)

35 And the same day, when the even was come, he
saith unto them, Let us pass over unto the other side.

36 And when they had sent away the multitude, they
took him even as he was in the ship. And there were
also with him other little ships.

37 And there arose a great storm of wind, and the
waves beat into the ship, so that it was now full.

38 And he was in the hinder part of the ship, asleep on
a pillow: and they awake him, and say unto him,
Master, carest thou not that we perish?

39 And he arose, and rebuked the wind, and said unto
the sea, Peace, be still. And the wind ceased, and there
was a great calm.

40 And he said unto them, Why are ye so fearful?
How is it that ye have no faith?

41 And they feared exceedingly, and said one to
another, What manner of man is this, that even the
wind and the sea obey him?

****** THE BREAKDOWN ******

When you really look at the passage that Mark tells in the story, we see that the disciples were terrified that the boat was going to be destroyed and everyone that was on it was going to die. While they were facing the storm, Jesus was asleep. They rushed over to Jesus and cry, "Teacher, don't you care if we drown?" Of course, Jesus quiets the storm with a word, but then he tells the disciples, "Why are you so afraid? Do you still have no faith?"

If we put this passage and apply this in our daily life, we would see that Jesus not only has power over the storms of life; but he experiences them alongside us, loves us, saves us from them and wants us to trust him more than we do. The storms don't worry Jesus. We must know that he's right there with us during them, but he's perfectly calm about them. Jesus never showed any signs of worry, not terrified nor impatient. In fact, he's so calm, he's asleep. To many of us, he seems like he's not around. Many times we even wonder why doesn't he get up and do something about the situations at hand. Sometimes, we even start to wonder does he even knows the trouble that we're in, does he actually care, or whether he can do anything about it. What we have to actually learn is despite everything the way it seems; Jesus is in complete control and we're safe in his hand.

- BACK TO THE STORY...

I could tell that my brother was stressed out due to the fact that everything was on him. Trying to manage a household being that he was now the only person working was overwhelming. The true faith challenge was when he lost his job in September of 2011. When that happened, we were on the verge of just giving up literally. I truly had thought that God had completely deserted us. Nothing went right at all and all these talks especially from pastors and folks saying, "Just have faith! Everything is going to work out fine" went right out the door. In November of 2011, we were evicted and didn't have anywhere else to go to, so it seemed anyway.

God Shows Up (The Fight Isn't Over)

With everything that went on in our life and almost seemed that there were no doors opening up for us, a miracle took place in our life at that moment. My mother did land a job and we ended up moving into a nearby hotel located in the city of Burlington.

We ended up staying at this hotel for two and a half weeks before we found a place to go. We lived on faith each and every night for two weeks because we was paying by the day and didn't know how we were going to come up with the payment each day. We were charged around $30-40 per night. God truly stepped in our lives at that moment by sending a very caring friend in our life to help us out. We didn't expect her to help pay a few days up in advance for us to stay there. This was a sigh of relief for all of us. Within a few short days, we were able to go from living in a hotel into a boarding house in Burlington, NC.

We managed to stick things out for a bit, and then I get a call from a dear friend. Her name is Candace. We met on MySpace in 2006. We've been inseparable ever since. She's like a sister that I've always wanted.

The first time that we actually met in person was back in 2007 when her mother paid for our entire trip to the Bahamas. We met on the highway when I was driving my PT Cruiser back then. Anyway, she called me and asked how everything was going. I told her that things were getting a little bit better but still no luck with finding anything on my end. Her and her mom talked and asked me to come up there to get back on my feet. In my heart, I just wanted to escape from Burlington and try my luck somewhere else. I was hoping that I could do a lot better there than I would have in Burlington, NC. Just one problem that I had which was the fact I was flat broke without a dime to my name. Once again I had to get my hustle on to leave the state of North Carolina. In a few short months, I've saved up enough money to finally leave North Carolina and was on my way to Kentucky.

The Move to Kentucky

In my heart, I knew that I deserve the very best and that I needed a break from North Carolina. I wasn't seeing much of anything and just got frustrated with it all. My best friend's mother told me that she could help me get a job there that was employing hundreds people. She had applied and set up an appointment for me while I was still in North Carolina. I was still staying at the hotel in Burlington, NC during that time. I remembered buying a couple of suitcases and getting everything that I needed for the trip. My sister was so excited for me to finally leave North Carolina; come to Kentucky to get a fresh start and get back on my feet again. Unfortunately, things kept coming up and I didn't make the trip right away. I kept doing what I had to so till I get up the money again to make the trip.

Goodbye North Carolina, Hello Kentucky

After four more long months and doing everything that I knew how to do to get the money up, I finally purchased my bus ticket and was on my way out of North Carolina. I gave both my mom and my brother a hug and boarded the bus. Before I left out, my mother told me that she wanted nothing but the best for me and that she prays that everything work out for me in Kentucky. I told her if everything pans out that I would help get her out of North Carolina.

My first stop was in Winston-Salem which was a very short wait. Afterwards, I ended up in Virginia in which I stayed almost 5 hours there before I moved on to Tennessee. I was in Chattanooga, TN but missed the direct bus to take me straight to Kentucky so I ended up getting on the Memphis, TN bus which resulted in a 5-6 hours layover. I finally boarded the bus that took me straight in Louisville, KY. I arrived into Louisville, KY around 7:00pm that Friday evening. The entire trip took me a day and a half to get to my destination. I got to say this; I finally saw why people call Kentucky the "Bluegrass State." At first glimpse, I thought it was for the birth of "Bluegrass Music" which wasn't the case. When I was on the bus looking out the window, I did notice that the grass had a bluish color tint to it. I did meet some interesting people on the bus. Some of the people that I met were coming from southern states such as Florida, Georgia, and a few from Alabama just for a better opportunity. When I had arrived at the Greyhound bus terminal, I was immediately picked up by my sister and her mother who is like a second mother far away from home. I remembered getting in her 2007 Cadillac Escalade Truck, in which is also my favorite SUV; heading back towards her home in Radcliff, KY. On the way going back to her home, we stopped by a local thrift store to get some winter clothes for me. Once we arrived in Radcliff, I ended up staying with my sister.

Life in Kentucky

I have to say that it felt really great living in Kentucky. I was thinking in the back of my mind that everything was going to be right this time around. I was going to get all the help and support needed to get me back to where I needed to be at in my life. Before I even left to come to Kentucky, I didn't even have a stable job, no car, barely any money, and no hope period. Being that I was with my sister and my other mother, they could help me get around the city being that they have cars to help me apply for jobs in the city of Radcliff, Elizabethtown, and Louisville. I was provided room and board and anything else I needed. I did notice that Radcliff, KY was very similar to my home in Burlington, NC. The only difference is that the town was more much smaller. I had gotten the chance to meet some of my sister's friends as well as other family members.

When the weekend rolls around, me and my sister would go out and really got to enjoy the town a bit.

I did get to experience a small taste of what Kentucky has to offer, but I never lost sight on why I was mainly there in the first place.

I also had gotten to spend time with my adopted nieces and nephew. I love them so much. They love calling me "Uncle Robert." I try my best to be the best uncle that I can be to them.

Jasmine *(Top Left)* **Samarah** *(Top Right)* ***Chris Jr.*** *(Bottom)*

When I was staying in Kentucky, I had applied for jobs at several places. Unfortunately, nothing turned around for me for quite some time. Even places that I've went to was pre-judging me from the start and never gave me a chance. It was so frustrating I felt like just quitting just because it got to the point that I'm facing the exact same issue that I was facing in North Carolina. Within a month's time, a job opening came up and I ended up working in Shepherdsville, KY at a factory making plastic bowls and plastic lids to be distributed in major retail stores such as Wal-Mart and Costco. I was working 12 hour days there and only for low pay. I was doing the best I could to perform well on that job, but my ADHD/ADD once again got in my way. I kept making so many mistakes and when I was getting yelled at by the supervisor saying, "What's wrong with you?" I just went completely off. I ended up losing that job after a full month of being there. Once again, I was right back where I started and began my search again. There was an opening at a company that distributed merchandises all over the world through online shopping. I went to apply for the position through a staffing company. I went down to the place where they done the hiring and interview at which took almost 4-5 hours. They were hiring people left and right; didn't even matter if you had something on your background. Anyone with a pulse got a job basically put it. I thought to myself, "Hey! I have a much greater shot with this than I had with anything else. I should have no problems here." It was a warm Tuesday morning when I stopped by there to apply. When I got finished with everything, I was given a schedule on when come in to work and other additional paperwork to fill out. I was excited about how everything was going, and then I get an unexpected phone call from the staffing agency. They told me that I was disqualified. This is how the phone conversation went.....

Staffing Agency*..."Hello. Can I speak to Robert Smith?*

Me*..."This is him speaking."*

Staffing Agency*..."The reason that we're calling you is because you recently came to the facility for a position for order puller."*

Me*..."Yes I have.*

Staffing Agency*..."Well, unfortunately you're been disqualified from this position at this time."*

Me*... (Short pause) "Well if I'm disqualified, then tell me the reason why. I deserve that much at least to be told what I'm being disqualified for. Just tell me the exact reason. Don't try to hide it from me.*

Staffing Agency*..."We can't give you a reason, but you can apply for other positions here that we have available if you like."*

Me... *No thanks! I won't be applying back any time soon. Bye*

I told my sister and her mother Della this news and they was in complete shocked. My sister thought and even said,

"Are you cursed?" and I replied back, "I don't know? I might be with all these things going on." Kind of reminded me of a scene from the movie "Friday" when Craig supposedly got fired on his day off.

I can only imagine how the conversation would have gone in my own life. It would probably go something like this with Pops saying, "That's stupid. How in the heck you get fired from a job you never even worked at? Man…you're worse than my son Craig" At first, it really did seem like nothing ever went my way. Della just started crying because of the fact I'm being mistreated and shunned out once again. Doesn't matter where I went I was being discriminated against and rejected once more. I think what really hurts the most is that all I wanted is to be treated fairly, but it just wasn't happening for me. A couple of months later, things were just going south for me and my sister. No income was coming in and we were just living on faith only. She gets a phone call from her husband, who at the time served in the United States Army. They began talking and she eventually told him that I was staying with her in Kentucky just to get back on my feet. He was stationed in Aberdeen, Maryland. She made plans to move to Maryland with her husband and asked him if it was ok for me to come to Maryland and stay with them until I found a job. He agreed to the request, but I didn't find out about it until May of 2012. When she came up to me and told me the news that I was moving to Maryland. I was like "Wow…another huge unexpected move?" Well if this is what it's going to take to get my life together then let's make this happen. Within the next month we were on our way to Maryland.

The Move to Maryland

We ended up spending the next few weeks packing and cleaning the apartment out. It was like moving an entire apartment all the way to another state 10 hours away. While we were getting ready for the move, I did meet my sister's husband for the very first time. When I was staying in Kentucky, I also found a church there in which I fell in love with. Everything was going well with the church I was attending. I felt like I was at home and I didn't want to go anywhere else at that moment. When it was time to get things together, I must say that in my heart I didn't want to leave that church but it was time to move on with things and begin again in a new place. When our pastor found out that we all was moving, he and his wife were shocked at first. They really didn't want us to move, but they agreed that maybe it was best for now. They were very nice people to be around. He and his wife took all of us out to dinner to fellowship for one last time. Afterwards we headed back to begin finishing up packing. Once we started packing the remaining items for the move and cleaning out everything else, my best friend's mother had gave me some word of encouragement and some cash for the road. She told me that I may have a much better opportunity in Maryland than

I ever had in Kentucky. She felt bad that nothing had worked out for me in Kentucky, but inspired me to press forward and never ever quit no matter how tough life gets for me. I simply told her this, "I will do my very best to hang in there and never quit." She gave me a hug and next thing you know, we're on our way to Maryland.

Our Arrival to Maryland

We ended up taking two vehicles going to Maryland. One of them was my sister's car and the other one was the moving truck. Her husband was driving the moving truck with me riding shotgun while her and the kids was in her car. We stopped in several places and got to see some incredible scenery. As we were traveling, her husband and I bonded for the purpose to get to know each other. Come to find out that we had very similar interests and dreams. We both had an open mind to make money in anything and every opportunity that came by. I really admire that. During that time in my life, I was searching for my own path to freedom. Ten hours later, we finally arrived in Aberdeen Proving Ground, Maryland. It was very late when we arrived and all of us were very exhausted from the long drive. We ended up retiring for the night and made plans to unpack in the morning. We were staying on base being that her husband was stationed there.

We got up bright and early to unload the moving truck. The one thing I hate most about moving is loading and unloading everything. Once we all got settled in I started my path on trying to find a job so I could be able to move my family from North Carolina and finally get them away from the nonsense there. It took me a month to find a job which was way less time it took me to find something in Kentucky and North Carolina combined. I worked for a company that shipped chocolate candy to schools everywhere in the United States through a staffing agency. The pay was great, but the hours wasn't. Another downside was that the job assignment only lasted three weeks. Once again while I was on that job, I was still getting picked on constantly. It almost seems like there was a dark cloud over me of some kind and it wasn't leaving me. There have been times where I honestly felt like nobody understands me at all. I remained at that job until the assignment ended which was within a month. After my job ended, I was moved to another job only for a week. Afterwards, I was once again out of work. This time around, I didn't let it get to me at all. I just continued on with things and just took everything one day at a time. During the month of August, we all were invited to go to the Baltimore Raven's Training Camp. Since Candace's husband served in the Military, we were able to get great seats. It was awesome just to go to the training camp. I got to meet some of the players and the cheerleaders.

It was really cool to see everyone having fun including the kids. They were so happy. This was back in 2012 when I went in which was also the last season that Baltimore Raven's own Ray Lewis was going to play. Afterwards, we went home and retired for the rest of the night. The following week later, I was back at it again just trying to find out what's my next move. I could tell that frustration was in the air and setting in especially from both my sister and her husband because things were not going well in my life and that nothing was breaking through for me. I was putting a strain on the family financially. Her husband had to go to training in Virginia during the second week of September, and he wanted me out on my own by then. I did get a job offer, but just when I was about to start work I had to decline it. The reason being was that time ran completely out for me and it was time to head back home again.

Going Back Home to North Carolina

When it came time for me to pack my bags and go back to North Carolina, I felt like my world ended. My biggest fear was heading back to a place where I never really had a real chance to make anything of myself. Even my sister saw my facial expression and she started talking to me and giving me some real advice. She told me this, "Bro I know it's not going to be easy. Maybe going back to North Carolina may just be what's best for you right now. This opportunity will only help develop you. I know society never gave you a "real chance." Just face the fear and have faith. I know that people have put you down and call you things that you're not. Just because people put a label on you doesn't mean that it's true. Everything is going to work out fine for you. I believe in you." I simply thank her for all the support and she always tells me that she will always have my back no matter what. One thing that I can say that I'm so blessed to have a woman like her in my life as far as having someone that is like a sister to me. I always wanted a sister and now I have one. I gave everyone one last hug and I ended up going with her husband back to North Carolina. When we were on the highway traveling, we popped in some great motivational CD's to listen to help us develop our mindset. Lord knew in my heart that I really needed it. As I was listening to what was being said, I quickly had a revelation about everything that went on up to that particular point in my life. I started to believe that God wanted me to go back there to take care of my mother, get myself together, overcome all the negativity in my life, and bring my family out as well as making an impact there in North Carolina. To me everything starts at home.

Chapter 6:
Back Home Again

The Road Trip Back Home

Before I had finally returned back home, we stayed in Virginia. I stayed there at least till that Saturday. My sister's husband had to attend to one of the schools for the Army there. I was in a hotel that was near the training facility. He showed me around the place. I have to say everything in Virginia was an experience. I do miss the complementary meals we had there at the hotel. He was giving me some advice on things that I should do while I'm in North Carolina and how to apply everything I learned in Maryland and in Virginia to help me get me where I needed to be at in life. When Saturday rolled around, we gassed up and were ready to make the trip to North Carolina. I had really dreaded going back to that place. Fear was kicking into overdrive and I was so stressed out about going back to North Carolina. I had in my mind even then that there were absolutely no opportunity for me whatsoever. The fear that I had was being in the same exact place and not going anywhere in life. I remembered what my life was when I was staying in North Carolina before I left and now going back to it just was unbearable to me. Somehow I gain enough courage to stick this out the best way I could.

Back in Burlington, North Carolina

I had finally arrived back in Burlington, North Carolina at the same boarding house that I was at with my mother and brother. They were happy to see me again. They have noticed that I lost weight. I was very happy to see them also. It was an incredible feeling seeing them, but I was very nervous about my direction in life in Burlington, NC. In the back of my mind, I was saying to myself this, "What's here for me?" I had no transportation still or anyway to get around. However, I did manage to save up $1,000 dollars from the jobs that I've worked for when I was out of state. The money had lasted for a while, but eventually that ran out and I was back to where I began at once again. I knew in my heart that something had to change and needed to change right now. I wasn't going to let my situation or let this town break me. My sister would check on me from time to time just to see how things are coming along with me. During my trying times or my "lean times", I was just taking things one day at a time and just knew that patience and faith was my only source to help me get through this entire transition in my life.

The House of Horrors

To those that have been where I've been or walked those familiar roads in life, you should know that coming from the streets of hard knocks is hard living. Life will not bend or break for anyone. I used to see my mother day after day work so hard just to see her have nothing to show for it.

The place that we were all staying at was a nightmare to say the least. If you've ever lived in boarding houses or know anyone that live in one, you know what usually goes down in places like that. All I would see is drug dealers or pushers coming in selling drugs to the drug addicts, prostitutes going in and out of the place, mentally ill people, and folks with felonies that couldn't go anywhere else staying at the boarding house. We were caught in all of it. Cops would be called almost every single day just to resolve disputes and sometimes would make arrests if needed. I wanted to get of this environment so bad that it became an obsession. I knew deep down inside that we deserve way much more than living in these "slums." More than that, I wanted my mom finally happy and not be in an environment like that ever. Most people that know me personally know that I usually kept to myself and respected other people's personal space. There have been times in the boarding house where I've gotten into several altercations with some of the tenants there. In situations like this, you don't have to look for trouble; trouble comes looking for you instead. I can say that being in what I call "The House of Horrors" really built my toughness from a mental standpoint. The reason why I say this is because I had to learn how to deal with all kinds of spirits. Another reason is because I had to "stand my ground" and prepare for anything and everything that came my way in that place.

When things got worst and I just couldn't take it any longer, I immediately told my mother that we got to leave this place before I lose my mind in this place. She simply agreed with the decision and how I felt about the place so we continued our search for a new place right away.

Trying To Find Hope & My Purpose

During the time we were trying to make a transition out of where we were living at into a much better place, I started evaluating everything that has taken place in my life. I had wondered to myself, "Is this it? Is this supposed to be my life? Is this is what my life is going to be? If this is so, then I really don't have anything else to look forward to any longer. My life is not worth living anymore." I was at that point of throwing in the towel because nothing else seemed to work for me. It felt like no matter what I've done or how hard I worked at something, it seems to fall apart. I've even cried out to our Lord and ask, "Why is this happening to me? What did I do to deserve all this negativity and torment in my life? I left my hometown of High Point, NC to get away from the very same thing that has haunted me ever since the time I was born and it seems like this won't leave me." I really just didn't understand anything anymore nor did anything make any sense at all.

Months went on by and I really didn't see anything changing in my life. On one particular day, I happen to run into a guy that I met when I was out getting lunch. His name was Thomas Dennis. At first we were talking about how messed up everything is in the world, then all of a sudden we began talking about Jesus Christ. I told him about some things that went on in my life and the frustrations that I've felt this entire time. He advises me that I needed to get back in church and seek God. He told me about the church he was attending to called World of Pentecost which is located in Burlington, NC. He also gave me the business card as well as his personal contact number to reach him. I took the card and placed it in my wallet and simply told him that I would come out and visit one day. A couple of months later, I ran into him again at the very same place. He asked me how everything was going in my life. I simply told him that everything is still the same. I really haven't seen any progress lately. He once again gives me an invitation to come to church and truly seek God. Of course I told him that I would visit the church, but never made the attempt. A month and a half later, I run into a lady whom I later found out was also a member of the exact same church that Thomas went to. She also told me that I needed to come to that church. She also stated to me that I will finally find what I'm looking for. Then I started looking into this situation a bit. I thought to myself, "I run into this guy on several occasions and now this lady comes to me with the same exact purpose in mind. They all wanted me to go to this church. Is God trying to get my attention using these people or what?" Another month goes by and I once again met Thomas. When I saw him this time around, I approached him and we started talking. I told him that I was sick and tired of my situation and really was trying to figure out everything. He was sharing with me testimonials from people that were in far worst situations than I was facing. After listening to him telling this story he simply asks me this question," Have you ever been baptized in Jesus name?" I told him, "I was baptized I think, but that has been years ago." He invited me to come to their revival and I accepted the invitation. I told him that I don't have transportation. He simply said, "That's ok. I can have someone from the church to come pick you up and take you there and back home." I had agreed to the offer and finally made my decision to go.

Chapter 7:
Turning Point

Re-Routing My Life (The True Turning Point)

There will be many times in your life where you will come to a fork in the road sort of speak and you will ask yourself, "What direction should I go?" In my heart, I wanted my entire situation to change. I was so sick and tired of all the negativity I was receiving in my life. When I was out and about, I would usually see couples whether married or not display their love and affection towards each other out in public. I would also see them with their kids. I truly wanted that. I wanted that so much because I know in my heart I deserved it. I also wanted to do something in my life that I can feel so happy and proud of doing. I was in search for my true purpose here on Earth. In a nutshell, I just wanted to live a fulfilled life. Keep in mind that I was still lost and was trying to find my way back. I knew the road that I was going on this entire time wasn't going anywhere. I also knew that if I kept going and continued on this path where

I've been traveling; my decisions would eventually destroy my entire life. When I made that decision to go to church and seek God for the answer, that's the moment where my direction in life shifted. The reason why I had stopped going to church was simply because I thought God abandoned me. With everything that has taken place in my life, I just thought I was a mistake. If you ever watched the show on TV called "Married with Children"; my luck was way worse than Al Bundy without the kids or the wife. I was determined to at least find hope again.

The church van had approached my home and I was on my way to World of Pentecost for the very first time. It was a revival that I ended up attending. The service was amazing. The speaker that delivered the message that night was from Alabama. I will never forget that message that he spoke that Monday night. The message was "Restoration." He pointed out that in order for things to work out in your life, you have to let go of everything in the past. You can't move forward while your mind is stuck in the past. Everything that happened in the past has happened for a reason. God can heal the hurt and give you the strength to carry on fulfilling your divine purpose. That message really hit home to me. I later figured out that the message that was being spoken wasn't just some coincidence. I believed in my heart that God wanted me to hear it and know that whatever I've endured all twenty plus years that He can completely turn everything around for me. I had to trust Him and know that Jesus Christ has everything under control. Later on that night I went to the altar to completely repent of all my sins and I also got baptized in Jesus name.

Acts 2:38 (KJV)

38 Then Peter said unto them, Repent, and be baptized every one of you in the name of Jesus Christ for the remission of sins, and ye shall receive the gift of the Holy Ghost.

Mark 16:16 (KJV)

16 He that believeth and is baptized shall be saved; but he that believeth not shall be damned.

John 3:16 (KJV)

16 For God so loved the world, that he gave his only begotten Son, that whosoever believeth in him should not perish, but have everlasting life.

John 3:5 (KJV)

5 Jesus answered, Verily, verily, I say unto thee, Except a man be born of water and of the Spirit, he cannot enter into the kingdom of God.

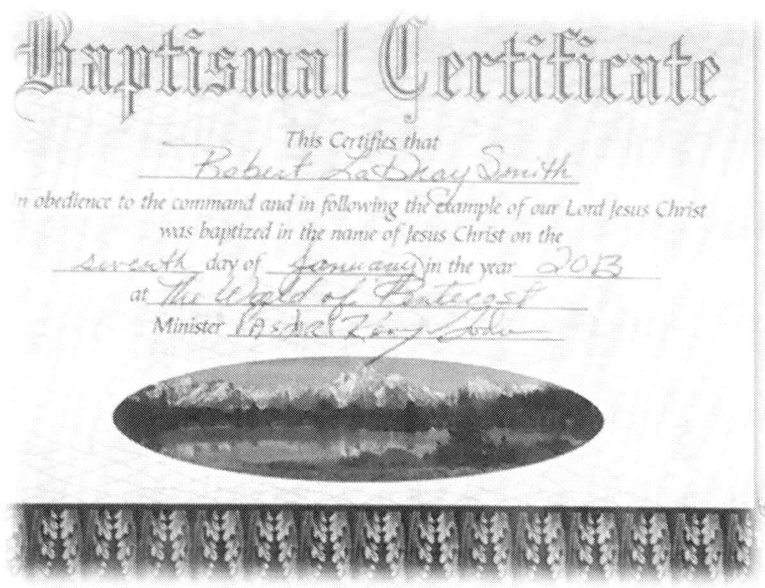

Baptismal Certificate

This Certifies that

[illegible] Smith

in obedience to the command and in following the example of our Lord Jesus Christ was baptized in the name of Jesus Christ on the

seventh day of January in the year 2013

at The World of Pentecost

Minister [illegible]

The thing that I've struggled with the most was forgiveness. I don't care who you are, even for those that are Christians will find it difficult to forgive someone especially when they done so much hurt to you emotionally, mentally, and physically. It almost feels like pouring battery acid on an old wound that will never heal up. It's hard facing the very same people that hurt you. I quickly realized that if I don't learn this step, unforgiveness would become a cancer in my life. In fact, not forgiving someone will eventually grow into something that can literally destroy you in the end. I knew that it's not going to be an easy journey in my faith walk with Christ. I do know that it's going to be a process just like everything else. I began to start down this path towards forgiveness and this was just the beginning of things turning around for me in my life.

.

Seeking God for Wisdom

I wanted to get rid of this negative stigma or "label" that was placed on me. Being that I grew up being misunderstood by many people, I knew that I'm a very bright and intelligent person. The problem was that nobody could see that about me. All people would see is a "big country boy that look slow." I went to God in prayer and asked Him to fill me up with wisdom, knowledge, and understanding of everything about Him.

Matthew 6:33

33 But seek ye first the kingdom of God, and his righteousness; and all these things shall be added unto you.

Matthew 7:7-8 (KJV)

7 Ask, and it shall be given you; seek, and ye shall find; knock, and it shall be opened unto you:

8 For every one that asketh receiveth; and he that seeketh findeth; and to him that knocketh it shall be opened.

The one thing that I love about serving God is that even though the world judges people accordingly on what they observe, God has a complete total different perspective. In my case, God didn't care what I had in my head. He only cares about what's in my heart. I was open-minded and humble enough to go to Him and ask him, and He did deliver on that promise.

My Journey Begins

I knew that in order for me to overcome everything that I've been facing, I must find my strength in the Word of God. I had to start getting into the Bible more and start going to church every chance I get to help recharge or "rejuvenate" my soul and put more knowledge in my head. At first, I didn't know where to even begin. I start making a list of the things that I've been dealing with for a long time (my weaknesses) and started finding Bible verses that went along with my situations. Afterwards, I began to work on them one by one until I overcame them. This is a concept that I've learned over the past few years, unless it's written down to where you see them, you will never accomplish anything you set your mind on doing. This is a sample of what I had written down.

My Biggest Obstacles/Challenges

My Problems	Bible Solutions
1. Lack of faith	Proverbs 3:5, 2 Corinthians 5:7, Hebrews 11:6, 1 John 5:4, Mark 9:23, Luke 17:6, Hebrews 11:1-39

2. Unforgiveness	Mark 11:25, Ephesians 4:26-27, Proverbs 24:17, Ephesians 4:32, Matthew 6:14-15
3. Low self esteem	1 Samuel 16:7, Song of Solomon 4:7, Philippians 4:13, Psalm 139:14, 1 John 3:1, 1 Peter 1:18-19
4. Anger	Ephesians 4:26-27, James 1:19-20, Proverbs 29:11, Proverbs 15:18, Proverbs 15:1, Proverbs 16:32
5. Impulsiveness	Proverbs 20:25-30, Ecclesiastes 5:2
6. No true guidance	Psalms 25:5 , Psalms 32:8, Psalms 37:23-24, Proverbs 3:5-

	6, Matthew 7:7, James 1:5-8

I'm going to break down some Bible scriptures here and also show you how I was able to apply them into my daily life. Keep in mind before I even started on my journey, I was completely lost and saw no future for myself. The lie was being told to me was so convincing that I literally believed them until I sought after God and his word. According to ***Matthew 6:33***; it clearly states, "But "seek ye first the kingdom of God, and his righteousness; and all these things shall be added unto you." In order to find your purpose here on Earth, you must seek Jesus Christ. Since I was so beating down from the torment I was getting from this life, I had to begin to build my faith back up. It's almost similar to a person "hitting the gym" after he or she has gained a lot of weight and then they begin to realize that their bodies are in serious danger of ruining their health. In order to build my faith level back up and get it up to speed, I began to turn to the book of Hebrews Chapter

11. To most Bible scholars, Hebrews Chapter 11 has been also referred to as "The Hall of Faith."

Many people whose names are listed there had various things said about their lives in regards to their own faith and their relationship with God. As a believer or even just someone who wants to build up any confidence in anything that you want to pursue, you can follow their stories and see the greatest demonstration of their acts of faith and perseverance. All the things that are mentioned about each person on what they've done in the course of their lives by faith could only be classed by God as their greatest acts of faith. As anyone start to read through the book of Hebrews chapter 11, you will see that all those people that mentioned, didn't always live a righteous life. They always had issues. Somewhere down the course of their lives, they made a conscious decision that causes them to walk by faith. The book of Hebrews chapter 11 is God's final assessment of their life. It's God's final word and the final say-so about their life. If you ever heard the old saying, "It isn't over till God says it's over", this is where that saying originated from. I'm going to give you some clear cut examples of the people that are listed that showed the greatest demonstration of faith.

Let's take a closer look at one of the original inductees Sarah and her life. According to ***Genesis 18***, you will begin to notice that the messenger had told Sarah that she was going to bear a child. In ***Genesis 18:12***, you will notice also that Sarah was laughing at the idea altogether. There were two things that hindered Sarah. She was too old and she couldn't conceive a child. At one point in her life, she had many doubts and even thought the idea of her even bearing a child was a complete joke. Somewhere in the course of her life between her fears and conception, faith arose in her heart. In the book ***Hebrews 11:11***, Sarah received strength to conceive and did indeed bear a child even past her prime years and said, "He that has promised, He is faithful."

Let's also look at Jacob and his life. Jacob never fit the description of being righteous or perfection. In fact, Jacob was not a great example of being a man with honor. Despite his ways, there was drive and determination that God saw and loved the man's attitude. God stated his love for Jacob in ***Romans 9:13***.

Romans 9:13 (KJV)

13 As it is written, JACOB HAVE I LOVED, BUT ESAU HAVE I HATED.

God loved Jacob's drive and determination, but hated his tactics he used. Jacob always took the wrong approach. He would never give God the opportunity to work things out in his life. Jacob was doing all the things he sees necessary in order to get the things he feels that was rightfully his. Jacob's early life wasn't marked by the acts of faith nor trust in God, but by fleshly efforts in order to accomplish the will of God. Somewhere in Jacob's life, there was a spiritual intervention and altercation that took place. Jacob had a one on one wrestling match with an angelic stranger that lasted throughout the night until the break of dawn ***(Genesis 32:24-30)***. During the fight, the stranger crippled Jacob with a blow to his hip that disabled him with a limp for the rest of his life. It was then Jacob knew what had happened. Jacob also understood it was only by God's grace and mercy he escaped from this episode with his life.

No man should be allowed to wrestle with God and live, but God was gracious.

Jacob would remember this event being conquered by God with every step he took for all the days of his life. This was a small price to pay for such a great gift. After the Lord touched him, he was no longer called Jacob, but was called Israel.

God leaves behind their past failures, doubts, short comings, and their faults. He emphasizes and enhances their faith. Keep this in mind; God doesn't look at your problems. He isn't looking at your failures, faults, short comings, doubts, or fears. Instead, His only concern for you is do you trust Him? Will you endure it and lean towards Him only? Will you allow yourself to put total faith in Him so He can do what's necessary to change the situation that's going on in your life?

I'm going to be honest with you, there will be times in your life when you're walking in faith that you will struggle. You will fall on your face repeatedly. There will also be times when life will push you to the breaking point. You will even start questioning everything around you and say to yourself, "Do I even have the will to survive this game called life?" There are those that have failed in their efforts to live for God. You must have faith, endurance, and the will to say, "I WILL MAKE IT NO MATTER WHAT LIFE BRINGS MY WAY."

Now let's take a closer look at Joseph and his story. Joseph was a man that went through turmoil most of his early life. His father made a coat for him of many colors **(*Genesis 37:3*)**. The coat represented the love and favor of his father. As time progresses, the coat was stripped from him **(*Genesis 37:23*)**. The coat was soaked in blood and was taken back to his father who made the father believe that a wild beast had consumed Joseph and killed him **(*Genesis***

37:32-35). The truth was that Joseph's brothers sold him into slavery (***Genesis 37:28***). Before he was sold off, his brothers threw him into a pit (***Genesis 37:23-28)***. The Ishmaelites purchased Joseph for twenty pieces of silver and then brought him to Egypt (***Genesis 37:28***). Later on in his life, he was sold once again to Potiphar, who is an officer of Pharaoh, the king of Egypt (***Genesis 37:36***). Joseph began moving up the ranks until he gained a leadership role and eventually ruled over all of Potiphar's possessions and everything that he owned. The Potiphar's wife takes a liking to Joseph and tried to seduce him (***Genesis 39:6-23***). Joseph refuses the temptation and flees. Potiphar's wife tells a lie telling every man that Joseph tried to rape her. Joseph is quickly arrested and sent to prison where he served many years. During that time, he made a decision in his life to do the very best that he can do to be the person he could be. He eventually becomes a keeper of the very same prison that he was once was a prisoner of ***(Genesis 39:22)***. The main point of this story is that all the things that went on in his life; every event that has taken place during his life was not always good. There was a lot of negativity involved in his life. There were things that came into his life that I'm very sure would drive any person to point of no return. Despite every negative effort being made, Joseph kept holding on to his faith. If you look at ***Genesis 50:15-20***, during that time in his life; Joseph confronts his brothers that did him nothing but harm to him. When they saw Joseph, they feared for their very life.

Genesis 50:15-20 (KJV)

15 And when Joseph's brethren saw that their father
was dead, they said, Joseph will peradventure hate us,
and will certainly requite us all the evil which we did
unto him.

16 And they sent a messenger unto Joseph, saying, Thy
father did command before he died, saying,

17 So shall ye say unto Joseph, Forgive, I pray thee
now, the trespass of thy brethren, and their sin; for
they did unto thee evil: and now, we pray thee, forgive

the trespass of the servants of the God of thy father. And Joseph wept when they spake unto him.

18 And his brethren also went and fell down before his face; and they said, Behold, we be thy servants.

Joseph wept and stated this in ***Genesis 50:19-20 (KJV)***

19 And Joseph said unto them, Fear not: for am I in the place of God?

20 But as for you, ye thought evil against me; but God meant it unto good, to bring to pass, as it is this day, to save much people alive.

At this point in his life, he was able to place the spirit of reconcile in his heart. With everything that has taken place in his life, all the negativity, and with all the traumatic events that has occurred; one could say that, "It wasn't his brothers that made him; it wasn't prison that made him, or Potiphar's wife that made him. It was God that made him into the man he was. God had full control over his life. God was directing the course of his life in every situation that came his way.

Let's take a very closer look at Job. Job was a man was blameless and upright, one who feared God and turned away from evil. He had in his possession 7,000 sheep, 3,000 camels, 500 yoke of oxen, and 500 female donkeys, and very many servants ***(Job 1:1-5)***.

There was a day were Job's faith was put to the ultimate test. This is what Satan says to God in the book of Job.

9 Then Satan answered the LORD, and said, Doth Job
fear God for nought?

10 Hast not thou made a hedge about him, and about
his house, and about all that he hath on every side?
Thou hast blessed the work of his hands, and his
substance is increased in the land.

11 But put forth thine hand now, and touch all that he
hath, and he will curse thee to thy face.

This is what God says in responses to the wager

12 And the LORD said unto Satan, Behold, all that he
hath is in thy power; only upon himself put not forth
thine hand. So Satan went forth from the presence of
the LORD.

God allowed Satan to fully test Job's faith but there was one stipulation to the wager. Satan was not allowed to kill him. When the wager was on, Satan went all out holding back nothing. As you keep on reading the book of Job, Satan begins to attack Job's wealth, possessions, and his children as seen in ***Job 1:13-22***.

13 And there was a day when his sons and his
daughters were eating and drinking wine in their
eldest brother's house:

14 And there came a messenger unto Job, and said,
The oxen were plowing, and the asses feeding beside
them:

15 And the Sabeans fell upon them, and took them
away; yea, they have slain the servants with the edge
of the sword; and I only am escaped alone to tell thee.

16 While he was yet speaking, there came also another,
and said, The fire of God is fallen from heaven, and
hath burned up the sheep, and the servants, and
consumed them; and I only am escaped alone to tell
thee.

17 While he was yet speaking, there came also another,
and said, The Chaldeans made out three bands, and
fell upon the camels, and have carried them away, yea,
and slain the servants with the edge of the sword; and
I only am escaped alone to tell thee.

18 While he was yet speaking, there came also another,
and said, Thy sons and thy daughters were eating and
drinking wine in their eldest brother's house:

19 And, behold, there came a great wind from the
wilderness, and smote the four corners of the house,
and it fell upon the young men, and they are dead;
and I only am escaped alone to tell thee.

20 Then Job arose, and rent his mantle, and shaved his
head, and fell down upon the ground, and
worshipped,

21 And said, Naked came I out of my mother's womb,
and naked shall I return thither: the LORD gave, and
the LORD hath taken away; blessed be the name of the
LORD.

22 In all this Job sinned not, nor charged God
foolishly.

With the first wave of attacks on Job, Job still remained steadfast and never gave in or cursed God. After this attempt has failed, Satan begins his second wave of attack, this time on Job's health ***(Job 2:1-13)***.

Job 2:1-13 (KJV)

1 Again there was a day when the sons of God came to present themselves before the LORD, and Satan came also among them to present himself before the LORD.

2 And the LORD said unto Satan, From whence comest thou? And Satan answered the LORD, and said, From going to and fro in the earth, and from walking up and down in it.

3 And the LORD said unto Satan, Hast thou considered my servant Job, that there is none like him in the earth, a perfect and an upright man, one that feareth God, and escheweth evil? and still he holdeth fast his integrity, although thou movedst me against him, to destroy him without cause.

4 And Satan answered the LORD, and said, Skin for skin, yea, all that a man hath will he give for his life.

5 But put forth thine hand now, and touch his bone and his flesh, and he will curse thee to thy face.

6 And the LORD said unto Satan, Behold, he is in thine hand; but save his life.

7 So went Satan forth from the presence of the LORD, and smote Job with sore boils from the sole of his foot unto his crown.

8 And he took him a potsherd to scrape himself withal; and he sat down among the ashes.

9 Then said his wife unto him, Dost thou still retain thine integrity? curse God, and die.

10 But he said unto her, Thou speakest as one of the foolish women speaketh. What? shall we receive good at the hand of God, and shall we not receive evil? In all this did not Job sin with his lips.

11 Now when Job's three friends heard of all this evil that was come upon him, they came every one from his own place; Eliphaz the Temanite, and Bildad the Shuhite, and Zophar the Naamathite: for they had made an appointment together to come to mourn with him and to comfort him.

12 And when they lifted up their eyes afar off, and knew him not, they lifted up their voice, and wept; and they rent every one his mantle, and sprinkled dust upon their heads toward heaven.

13 So they sat down with him upon the ground seven days and seven nights, and none spake a word unto him: for they saw that his grief was very great.

This is my understanding on what Job was trying to say:

"Despite everything that went on in my life, I'm not going to give Satan any credit. I'm going to give God the credit. I know that God got everything under control. God's hand is upon my life."

If you have learned anything from each of these people that I have given an example of, it would be to never lose hope or your faith no matter how hard things may seem. God is in full control of everything.

Chapter 8:
Taking Back Control of My Life

The True Mindset of an Alchemist & a Blacksmith

When I started doing some research about ADD/ADHD and the people that have it, all I would see is the negativity surrounding the so-called "disorder." There wasn't much being said about the "disorder" in a positive note. In my eyes, there are great qualities of having ADD/ADHD that I'm going to go over with you. For starters, people with ADD/ADHD see things in an entire completely view than the average person. We're only interested in things that only interest us. We're very innovative, creative, and brilliant human beings. I wanted to share that with many people about it so that you will have a very clear understanding on the benefits of the "disorder."

Have you ever heard of an "alchemist?" If not, it's clearly ok The book definition, alchemy is a form of chemistry and speculative philosophy practiced in the Middle Ages and the Renaissance and concerned principally with discovering methods for transmuting baser metals into gold and with finding a universal solvent and an elixir of life. Someone who's an alchemist is a person that can transmute a common substance, usually of little value, into a substance of great value. I honestly think in my heart that those that have ADD/ADHD are somewhat considered to be "nature's alchemist" because we're able to take things or see life's problems and turn them into opportunity to where we're in position to help others as well as benefiting ourselves. I consider having ADD/ADHD as a gift because if it wasn't for it, I couldn't use my creativity or innovativeness to create this book or find ways to get this book out to you and fulfill my God-given purpose here on Earth.

If I really wanted to fully maximize my "gift" which is the ADD/ADHD, I must really learn naturally how to manage and enhance it. What I mean by enhancing my "gift" is that I must continue to sharpen my mind with full knowledge.

Just like how a "blacksmith" wields metal to make it sharp and sturdy to where it can cut through any material and still stay intact. I had to sharpen my mind to cut through all the negativity that people try to corrupt my mind with and keep me on the ground instead of ascending to higher heights in life. The way that I was sharpening my mind was reading the Bible. Then from there I began listening to a lot of personal development CD and audiobooks. This was my very first step to reprogramming my mindset.

Discovering the Power From Within

"If you're so far in the hole (stuck in your situation) that you're seeing all your dead relatives; then you know it's time for change."

~ R.L. Smith

Let me begin by asking you these questions. Do you truly want to live a life on your own terms? What I mean by that is this. Do you really want to become financially free, be truly happy, have great health, and have the nicer things in life? Do you even want to see changes within your home, your career, church, or any other area in your life? Do you want to finally attract your soul mate in your life or fix your relationship that you're already in? Do you have a very strong desire to have a much better job? Do you have a desire to boost your self-confidence, your self-esteem, and help others do the same? If this is the case, then you really need to listen to what I have to say.

The first step towards changing your life is changing your mindset. God wants to change the way we think and the way we live. God never intended for His children to go lacking of anything, live a life of limitation, being poor, or live a very unfulfilled and hopeless existence. If you want a clear book definition on what "mindset" is it's the way you believe, think, and feel about yourself, your life, and everything that comes your way on a daily basis.

Everything that you ever believed in, heard, even seen from your own eyes and values that you hold within your heart is the result of your mindset. I'm going to give you a clear cut example on how powerful this step is and why you must do all the necessary steps to change your way of thinking. If a person grows up not receiving any love or emotional support they truly needed to get them through life, the result of that would be that their self-image and their self-esteem will be destroyed. As time progresses on, it will make the individual feel unloved, worthless, and feel that they don't count or fit in this society. For an example, most inmates that you see in jail or in prison didn't decide to grow up and become what they are. Most of them may have faced traumatic events in their life that led up to where they're at today. It could range from mental, physical, or sexual abuse that has gone unnoticed; they may have been tormenting for a long period of time and had bottled it up, or they probably felt neglected. I know this very well because I felt this way for over the past 30 years of my life. I had experienced abandonment, mental and physical abuse, and had been tormented, shunned, and even put down by nearly everyone I came in contact with within the course of my life. When I was denied every opportunity that came my way in my life such as job offers, relationships with women, and sometimes even making new friends; I felt like I was worthless and didn't even belong here on Earth. It didn't matter how hard I try to make things right or do things that's going to help me, all I would do is mess things up and run people away from me. At one point, I thought my life was cursed. I knew that I had to make some kind of change right away because if I didn't change my mindset right away, it would chase off any good opportunity that would come my way. Being that I had acknowledged that everything that I was going through was unacceptable, I began changing my thought process by saying positive affirmations. This was my affirmation that I kept saying to myself.

"I am a thought conceived by God. I was formed in his image and when I was born, He placed into me a piece of Him. I know I was wonderfully crafted by Him. He has a divine purpose for my life and I'm going to walk in my birthright."

I kept reminding myself this every single day. By saying this affirmation, this help shifted my way of thinking and kept me in total alignment with God and His will for my life. I highly recommend anyone that's trying to change their way of life to start speaking life into your situation if you're not doing so already. I'm going to give to you some affirmations that you can start applying right now to change your thinking pattern, especially when it comes to self-esteem. You can pick and choose anyone you like, but the idea of this exercise is to help gain control back into your life.

Examples of Affirmations You Can Apply In Your Life

* *I am unique and special.*

* *Nobody on earth is exactly like me.*

* *I am chosen.*

* *My life has purpose and meaning.*

* *God created me in His own image.*

* *I am happy with the way I am.*

* *I appreciate my unique qualities.*

* *I am confident.*

* *I feel good about myself.*

* *I am seen as being very good.*

* *I am grateful to be me.*

* *I am born and destined to win!*

* *I am God's workmanship.*

* *I am designed for greatness!*

* *There are many positive qualities about me.*

* *God's hands have made me, and fashioned me.*

** I am made to be exceptional.*

** I am considered to be a treasure.*

** I am very valuable.*

** With God, all things are possible.*

** My life can be what I want it to be.*

** I am fearfully and wonderfully made.*

** I am a miracle.*

** I was born to succeed.*

** I am part of a chosen generation.*

** God has called me out of darkness into His marvelous light.*

** I am called to be a light to the world.*

** Just as I am - I am loved!*

** God loves me with an everlasting love.*

** I am thankful that my life is filled with favor and blessings.*

These Bible verses will help bring life into your spirit to win in this game called life.

Luke 10:1 (KJV)

1After these things the Lord appointed other seventy
also, and sent them two and two before his face into
every city and place, whither he himself would come.

Luke 10:17:20 (KJV)

17 And the seventy returned again with joy, saying,
Lord, even the devils are subject unto us through thy
name.

18 And he said unto them, I beheld Satan as lightning
fall from heaven.

19 Behold, I give unto you power to tread on serpents
and scorpions, and over all the power of the enemy:
and nothing shall by any means hurt you.

20 Notwithstanding in this rejoice not, that the spirits
are subject unto you; but rather rejoice, because your
names are written in heaven.

We must understand this; God is the Supreme Being and Creator of this world and the universe. He has all the power and authority. He also gave all of us the power to overcome Satan's deceptions and spiritual attacks for those that truly believe.

Our Spiritual Bloodline Heritage (Spiritual Ancestors)

This came from a devotional that I've found online from Pastor Solomon Aroboto of Christian Community Church Arklow.

Exodus 12:13 - *"And the blood shall be to you for a token upon the houses where ye are: and when I see the blood, I will pass over you, and the plague shall not be upon you to destroy you, when I smite the land of Egypt"*

That old saying that you will hear sometimes from people, "It's in our blood" isn't just some "old "saying. There's a powerful meaning to that phrase. A person's bloodline is their lineage. A person's lineage grants them access to into different areas in one's life what others have been restricted from. The book of ***Ephesians*** read as follows:

Ephesians 2:12-13 (KJV)

12 That at that time ye were without Christ, being
aliens from the commonwealth of Israel, and
strangers from the covenants of promise, having no
hope, and without God in the world:

13 But now in Christ Jesus ye who sometimes were far
off are made nigh by the blood of Christ.

By us being situated in Christ opens the door that had been in time past shut. Basically, the blood of Jesus is the key to every door in life. There is a demarcation in the realm of the spirit, which is the bloodline. The life of a thing is in its blood; hence, our guarantee to eternal life staying under the blood.

In today's world, it's unfortunate to see a lot of believers suffering so much lack, pain, ill health, tragedy, defeat, shame, and torment. Do you ever wonder the reason why a lot of true believers suffer? It is because they lack spiritual education in the power that is in the blood and name of Jesus. The blood line describes a spiritual separation of those marked with Christ and those not. There is a demarcation in the physical world between the rich and the poor, the young and the old, and male and female. The bloodline separates those that enjoy the benefits of the blood of Jesus from others. The power of the blood line in this case is the power of the blood based on our choice to remain under the covering of Jesus Christ.

People tend to give up their legal rights when they walk outside of God's word. We need to understand that the enemy is walking in the earth realm by permission so he is not allowed to cross the line because the blood line is beyond his jurisdiction. The scriptures refer to the devil as the prince of this world; however, the blood of Jesus keeps him off you (your property, family, job, business, life, health, marriage etc.). When we are under the blood line, we are in a place God shields; hence, the devil can't find us. We become invisible and unstoppable. The devil in lieu of this however seeks to strip the believer of their divine security and protection in the blood of Jesus by luring such out of the blood line. He tosses bait with pseudo prosperity (Cares of this world) which includes fame and worldly wealth. He depresses others through trials and tribulations (Wiles of the devil). The purpose of the devil doing all these is to shift us from our covering (The blood of Jesus). We must however understand that our being properly spiritually located is what will cause our relocation to the next level in the physical. Let's take a look into ***Ecclesiastes***.

Ecclesiastes 10:8 (KJV)

8 He that diggeth a pit shall fall into it; and whoso
breaketh a hedge, a serpent shall bite him.

Breaking the hedge is referenced to breaking out of the bloodline. When the hedge is broken, we are now being put under the threat of spiritual irrelevance, which leads to a physical stagnancy. Only those who are rooted and grounded under the power of the blood will flourish.

To back that statement up, let's look at the book of ***Psalm***.

Psalm 92:13 (KJV)

13 Those that be planted in the house of the LORD shall flourish in the courts of our God.

For more proof, let's look go back to ***Genesis***.

Genesis 47:27-28 (KJV)

27 And Israel dwelt in the land of Egypt, in the country of Goshen; and they had possessions therein, and grew, and multiplied exceedingly.

28 And Jacob lived in the land of Egypt seventeen years: so the whole age of Jacob was an hundred forty and seven years.

A long as the children of Israel remained in Goshen, they enjoyed peace and tranquility. Goshen was simply a shadow of how God wants us to remain located under the blood of Jesus. As long as we are spiritually grounded; no rain, flood or wind would be able to blow us away.

Some people willingly leave the blood line because of the feeling of entrapment. The blood does not entrap us; rather, it ensures and guarantees our freedom in Christ Jesus. As long as we are under the blood, the blood will keep speaking better things on our behalf in the name of Jesus.

When you are confronted by a difficult situation, you have the blood that is speaking open heavens on your behalf.

BENEFITS OF REMAINING UNDER THE BLOOD LINE

- Spiritual intimacy with God. ***Ephesians 2:13***
- The believer will flourish within and without. ***Psalm 92:13***
- Oppression will be far from us. ***Isaiah 54:14***

- We will enjoy divine and physical protection ***Psalm 91:1***
- The blood will speak better things on our behalf.
- Justification and salvation from wrath. ***Romans 5:9***

Awaken.... (A True Warrior Is Born)

"I took a stand and complete authority over my adversaries when I decided I wasn't going to fall prey or become a victim to the world's view about who I am. I will and always continue to fight it through God's words."

~ R. L. Smith

I had to sit back for a moment and take a closer look at the things that took place in my life, and what it took to overcome every situation. I wanted to break completely free from all the negativity around me, but found it being very difficult because it seemed like everything was coming at me at one time and there were no way to dodge the obstacles. Where I began to find the strength, the truth of who I am and who I truly belong to, and wisdom was by reading the Bible. When I began my journey, I noticed that there were people that are listed in there before our time had faced challenges from the likes that we've never have imagined. To begin developing my strength and courage, I started reading about the life of King David, King Solomon, Queen Esther, Moses, Samson, and more of other people as well.

King David's Full Story

When we look at his story, we see that King David was a man of contrasts. He was so totally committed to God, yet he was also guilty of some of the most serious sins ever to be written down in the Old Testament. David had lived a very difficult and frustrating life. From the very beginning, he was considered the "underdog" compared to his brothers. Always been overlooked and shunned. As time progressed on, he was constantly on the run from a very jealous and vengeful King Saul. Even when was crowned king of Israel, he was always engaged in combat to defend the kingdom. He was a great military leader and conqueror, but even he had issues conquering himself. He had a one night stand with Bathsheba, who was the wife of Uriah the Hittite. That affair ended up having disastrous consequences in his life. King David did fathered Solomon who later became one of Israel's greatest kings. He also fathered Absalom, who winded up rebelling and brought nothing but bloodshed and grief.

When you look at the life he lived, you will notice that his life was always a constant roller coaster ride. However, King David left all of us an example of his love for God and dozens of psalms, which were some of the most sincere and touching poetry ever written in our lifetime.

King David's Legacy

David had slain Goliath, champion of the Philistines, when David was only a youth and Goliath a giant and veteran warrior. David was victorious because he trusted in God for the victory, not himself. He killed many of Israel's enemies in battle.

Despite several opportunities, David refused to take out King Saul, God's first anointed king, who was pursuing David out of mad jealousy.

He became friends, like brothers, with Saul's son Jonathan, setting a model of friendship that everyone can learn from. King David is included in the "Hall Of Faith" in Hebrews 11.

David was an ancestor of Jesus Christ. Jesus was often called "Son of David." God called David a man after his own heart.

King Solomon's Full Story

King Solomon was the wisest man who ever lived and also became one of the most foolish. God gave him a gift of supernatural wisdom. Solomon ended up throwing it all away by disobeying God's commandments.

Solomon was the second son of King David and Bathsheba. His name means "peaceable." Even as a baby, Solomon was loved by God.

There was a conspiracy to rob Solomon of the throne orchestrated by Adonijah, who is Solomon's half-brother. Solomon knew that as long as Adonijah have lived, he would continue to connive and plot against Solomon in order to take the throne. Solomon had no choice but to take Adonijah out along with anyone that supported him in order to take the kingship. For those that read the passage, this act may seem brutal in our day, but back then you had to do what's necessary.

God appeared to Solomon in a dream and promised him anything he asked. Solomon chose understanding and discernment. God was so pleased with the request that he granted it, along with great riches and power.

Solomon's downfall began when he married the daughter of the Egyptian Pharaoh to seal a political alliance. He could not control his lust. Among Solomon's 700 wives and 300 concubines were many foreigners, which angered God. The inevitable happened: They lured King Solomon away from Yahweh into worship of false gods and idols.

Over his 40-year reign, Solomon did many great things, but he succumbed to the temptations of lesser men. The peace a united Israel enjoyed, the massive building projects he headed, and the successful commerce he developed became meaningless when Solomon stopped pursuing God.

King Solomon's Legacy

Solomon built the very first temple on Mount Moriah in Jerusalem which was a seven-year task. It was later would become one of the wonders of the ancient world. He also built a majestic palace, gardens, roads, and government buildings. He accumulated thousands of horses and chariots. After securing peace with his neighbors, he built up trade and became the wealthiest king of his time.

He is credited with writing much of the book of Proverbs, the Song of Solomon, the book of Ecclesiastes, and two psalms.

Samson's Full Story

To give you a glimpse of Samson's life, he stands alone as one of the saddest figures in the Old Testament. Sampson was a person who started with great potential, but selfishly squandered it all away with self-indulgence and sinful living. Despite his way of living, he is listed in the Hall of Faith in Hebrews 11, honored alongside Gideon, David, and Samuel. In the last moments of his life, Samson returned to God, and God answered his prayer.

Samson's birth was a miracle on its very own. His mother was barren (which means "not producing or incapable of producing an offspring"), but an angel appeared to her and said she would give birth to a son. He was to be a Nazirite all his life. Nazirites were those that took a vow to avoid drinking wine, cutting their hair, or being in contact with dead bodies.

When Sampson reached adulthood, his lust begins to overtake him. He married a Philistine woman, from the pagan conquerors of Israel. This led him into a confrontation in which he started killing Philistines. On one occasion, he took up the jawbone of a donkey and killed 1,000 men.

Instead of honoring his vow to God, Samson found a prostitute. The Philistines immediately took notice of his lustful desires and got a woman named Delilah to not only to seduce him, but to learn the secret of his great strength. Samson told her it was in his long hair which was a very big mistake on his part.

They cut his hair, gouged out his eyes, and made Samson a slave. After a long time of excruciating pain, Samson was put on display during a feast to the Philistine god Dagon. As he stood in the crowded temple, Samson positioned himself between two pillars.

He prayed to God to give him strength for one final act. It was later discovered that it's never been Samson's long hair that was the source of his power; it had always been the Spirit of the Lord coming upon him. God answered his prayer that moment. Samson pushed the pillars apart and the temple crashed down, taking out 3,000 enemies of Israel including himself. That act was later coin phrased as "Making his worst day his ultimate best day."

Samson's Legacy

He was dedicated as a Nazirite, a holy man who was to honor God with his life and provide an example to others. Samson used his physical strength to fight Israel's enemies. He led Israel for 20 years. He is honored in the Hebrews 11 Hall of Faith.

Queen Esther's Full Story

Esther lived in ancient Persia about 100 years after the Babylonian captivity. When her parents died, the orphaned child was adopted and raised by her older cousin Mordecai.

One day the king of the Persian Empire, Xerxes I, threw an extravagant party. On the last day of the festivities, he called for his queen, Vashti, to eagerly flaunt her beauty to all his guests. The queen refused to appear before Xerxes. Filled with rage, he had Queen Vashti removed from her position forever. At moment, Xerxes was on a mission to find his next queen. Xerxes hosted a royal beauty pageant and Esther was chosen for the throne. Her cousin Mordecai became a minor official in the Persian government of Susa.

Soon after, Mordecai uncovered a plot to assassinate the king. He then told Esther about the conspiracy to kill the king. Esther then reports this to Xerxes, giving credit to Mordecai. The plot was interrupted and Mordecai's act of kindness was preserved in the chronicles of the king.

At this same time, the king's highest official was a wicked man named Haman. He hated the Jews and he especially hated Mordecai, who had refused to bow down to him.

So, Haman devised a scheme to have every Jew in Persia killed. The king bought into the plot and agreed to annihilate the Jewish people on a specific day. Meanwhile,

Mordecai learned of the entire plan and shared it with Esther, challenging her with these famous words according from ***Esther 4:13-14***:

Esther 4:13-14 (KJV)

13 Then Mordecai commanded to answer Esther, Think not with thyself that thou shalt escape in the king's house, more than all the Jews.

14 For if thou altogether holdest thy peace at this time, then shall there enlargement and deliverance arise to the Jews from another place; but thou and thy father's house shall be destroyed: and who knoweth whether thou art come to the kingdom for such a time as this?

Esther urged all of the Jews to fast and pray for deliverance. She then begins taking matters into her own hands by risking her own life. The brave young Esther approached the king with a plan of her own.

She invited Xerxes and Haman to a banquet where eventually she revealed her Jewish heritage to the king, as well as Haman's diabolical plot to have her and her people killed. In a rage, the king ordered Haman to be hung on the gallows, which was the very same gallows Haman had built for Mordecai.

***** KEEP THIS IN MIND *****

Do you remember that old saying "Give a man enough rope and he will eventually hang himself?" Do you remember this one as well "Trying to dig a ditch for me and you will be the one lying in it instead?" This story hits it right on the head.

Mordecai was promoted to Haman's high position and Jews were granted protection throughout the land. As the people celebrated God's tremendous deliverance, the joyous festival of Purim was instituted.

Queen Esther's Legacy

This crisis transforms Esther from an easily controlled and submissive girl into a courageous leader. By taking charge of Mordecai's effort to stop Haman, she devises a risky plan that uses her wit, beauty, charm, and her judgment from a political standpoint to save her people. In doing so, she reveals her true identity as both a Jew and a woman of action, and shows us how we all can utilize our talents, strengths, and our brains to change the course of history. She had put the true meaning to the phrase, *"Use what your daddy (God) gave you."*

Moses's Story

Moses stands as the most dominant figure of the Old Testament. God chose Moses to lead the Hebrew people out of slavery in Egypt and mediate his covenant with them. Moses handed down the Ten Commandments, and then completed his mission by bringing the Israelites to the edge of the Promised Land. There were many issues that were very conflicting to Moses. If anyone were to look at the problem he had, you would learn that Moses had a speech impediment. The world would look at him and consider him "slow or retarded", but God worked mightily through him, supporting Moses every step of the way.

Moses's Legacy

Moses helped free the Hebrew people from slavery in Egypt, the most powerful nation in the world during that era. He led this huge mass of unruly refugees through the desert, kept order, and brought them to the border of their future home in Canaan. Moses received the Ten Commandments from God and delivered them to the people. Under divine inspiration, he authored the first five books of the Bible: Genesis, Exodus, Leviticus, Numbers, and Deuteronomy. His story redefines the meaning *"Slow people can rule a nation."*

When I went through each of their stories, I immediately saw the characteristics they had that I also possess within myself. Despite the things that that went on in my life, I never had fell victim to the world's way of dealing with battles that I've faced on a constant basis. I didn't turn to drugs of any kind, did not turn to drinking, or put a gun to my head to pull the trigger to end my life. By turning to the Word of God for the answer, I've found my God-given strength and now a newly renewed mindset to tackle and overcome many of life's challenges.

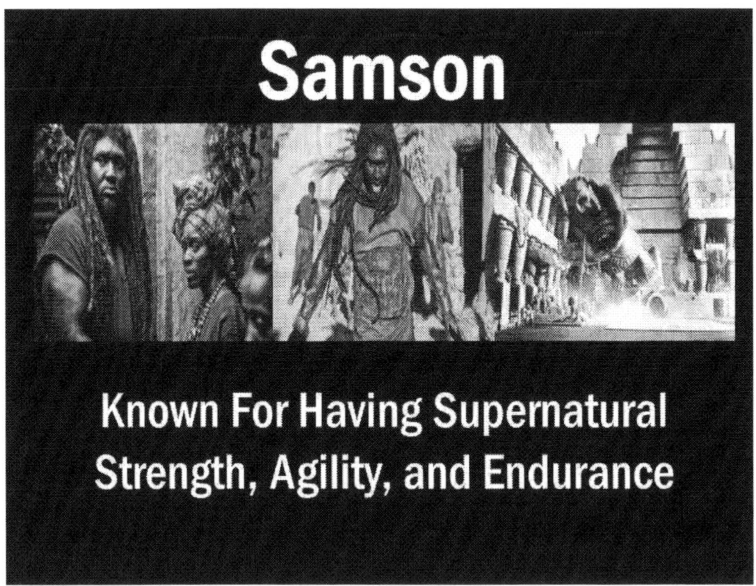

By the mighty hand of God, I'm able to move mountains in my life that seems impossible to move. Also with the endurance that I've gained, I'm able to endure and withstand anything problems that life throws my way.

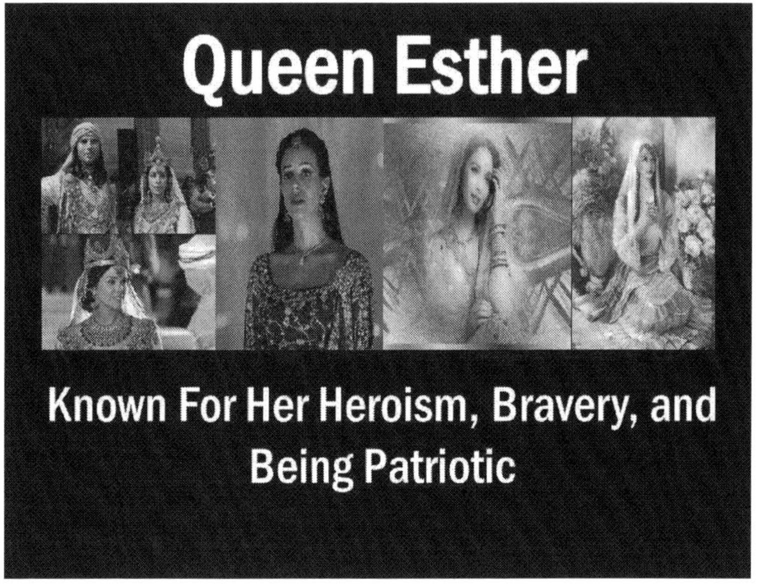

With the genuine love that God placed in my heart, I'm able to show compassion and a love for people to not only share my story, but to show many people who are completely lost or those that love the Lord, but don't know their purpose and future the way to find their divine purpose through this book and through speaking engagements, and other mediums.

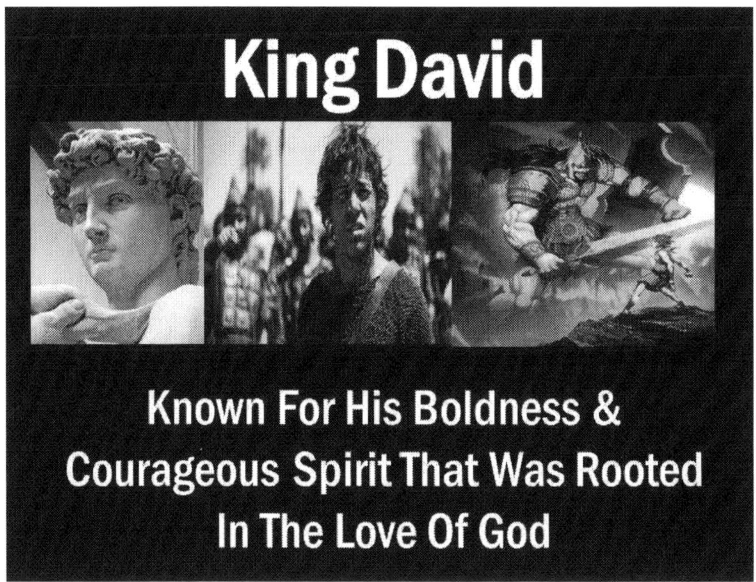

With my newfound strength; I have the courage and the boldness to stand up against those that have tried to trespass against me, Satan's lies and deception of who I am really am, and the world's judgment and views against me.

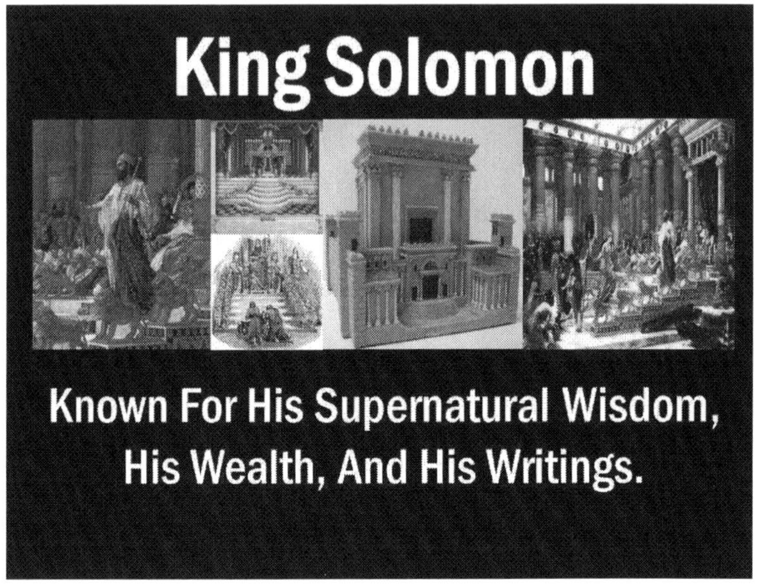

With God's help, I now possess great wisdom and intellect that not only I can use to help guide me on the right path in the journey of life and tackle some of life's difficult problems, but I can share this knowledge to many people that's having a very hard time trying to understand obstacles and problems that seem impossible to solve on their own.

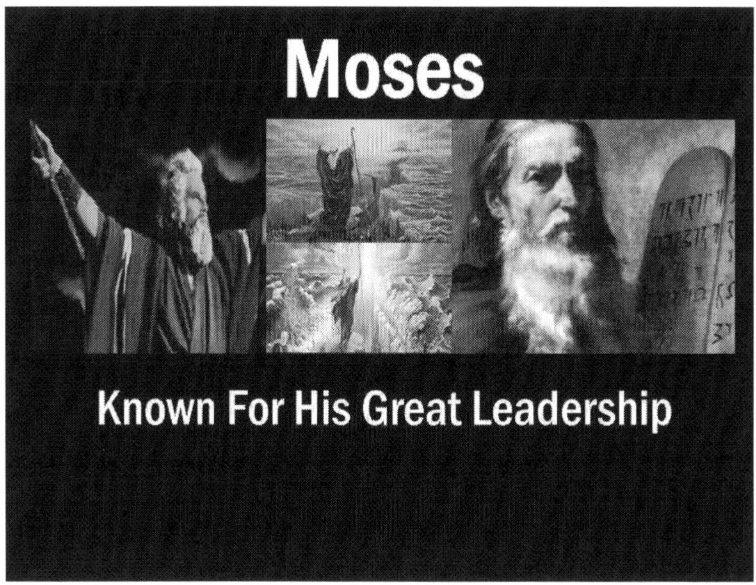

Even though I some similar flaws as Moses had, I have the God-given ability within me to lead many people towards Jesus Christ and finally break free people who have been "enslaved" in their own minds that many people had believed over time that they could never break free from the mindset of poverty, ill health, drugs, fear, despair, and a hopeless & fruitless existence.

The best thing about all of this is that we all within our bloodline possess these traits. It's in in our spiritual DNA.

God made us to excel in life, not to fail. You must learn how to use this towards your advantage in this life in order to exceed beyond the limitations that you or society has placed on yourself. It's time to unlock the "warrior" from within.

Life Gives Us a Mathematical Formula

You probably been going through a period of time in this life feeling like everything is set on autopilot and that you have no control over things that's going on in your live. Regardless of the situation, you have the power and authority to change what's going on in your life. In fact, there is a "real mathematical" equation to life. This may seem odd or you may say to yourself this, "Oh yeah right!?" I'm going to be very blunt here and tell you yes there is and what I'm going to show you is the formula you can start applying now to begin the paradigm shift towards a much better "YOU."

FORMULA TO LIFE

YT + YA + YR = YO/YL

The above formula that you see stands for this:

YT = Your Thoughts
YA = Your Actions
YR = Your Response
YO = Your Outcome
YL = Your Lifestyle

You must realize that everything that happens in your life starts with you and your thoughts. The way it goes is just like this:

- Your thoughts dictate your action.
- Your action dictates and forms your habits.
- Your outcome is the final result of all the decisions that you made leading up to the event.
- Your lifestyle is the end result of everything that took place in the process of your thinking.

Does this make total sense to you? This is the exact blueprint formula that is taken place in all areas of your life which includes financials, career choice, your love life, and the relationships you build with other people and so forth. I'm going to even go further and give you real life scenarios on how this formula is being applied so this can give you a much better perspective on things and how you can start shifting your mindset to focus more on the positive side of things instead of all the negativity.

GOOD EXAMPLES OF THIS FORMULA WORKING FOR YOU

1st Example

A young woman in her mid-20 has a very strong desire of having a family. She has been thinking about this moment for quite some time. As a matter of fact, she has been thinking about this ever since she began playing with dolls and easy bake ovens as a child. The woman has even taken things to the next level and already picked out the name of the baby. The only thing that's missing is a suitable mate. This is what's called the "thinking and creating" process. The young lady starts her search on finding a suitable mate by creating an online profile on various social networking sites and on some online dating sites detailing out everything about her and what she's looking for. This is the "action" process to get her towards that goal or dream. The young lady is getting many inquiries from her profile, but she's sitting through and weeding out all the ones that didn't make her "Top List" and focuses more on the guys that fit her description on what she's looking for. Afterwards, she begins by setting up dates with them. This is also part of the "action" process. Now, at this stage is where "patience and timing" kicks into overdrive. After going out with the guys that she saw suitable, this is the point where she has evaluated each person and sit down to see exactly what she likes, dislikes, and whether she sees herself with one of the guys. Even when she has made her choice on who she truly wants, they both have to have the same goal of a long-term relationship possibly marriage and not some "WHAAM BAAAM THANK YOU MA'AM.....I'm Gone!" mentality. The young lady has finally found her match and eventually gets married. She finally gets pregnant, thus a child is now being created. So now you see the formula is being implemented.

2nd Example

Let's say that you're in a career that you feel that it's not going anywhere for you. You hate the commute, the boss, employees, maybe it's the money, or you're just not getting the push you need. So you have a desire to earn more money to help you regain back control and finally leave your dead-end job. The issue is that you don't know who to do just that. So you sit down and you begin writing out your goals. You write out clearly that you want to make or earn at least $100,000+ per year in income (Breaks down to ***$10,000+*** per month). Now, the desire and the goal have been written down and you see this in plain view. The next step is figuring out how to do just that. This is where the "action" step kicks in. You start to do a self-evaluation on the things that interest you the most. You find out what your passions are and you discover how to turn that passion into profits. This is the first phase to the "action" part of the process. The next step for you is learning how to share or "distribute" what you have to the world. You begin to learn the basics of marketing and in that time you're on your way to earning the amount of money that your heart desire.

Once you got that down, begin to take action, and start being consistent with it; you will immediately see the results of your hard work. At that point, you can finally enjoy the lifestyle that you dreamed of having. All through this process, you learned how to take full advantage of untapped markets and leveraging your time and money which is the key components of wealth. This is the final part of the equation called the "Outcome & Lifestyle" process.

BAD EXAMPLES OF THIS FORMULA WORKING AGAINST YOU

Let's say that you're driving down the road and a cop gets behind you. Keep in mind that the cop may just be heading in the same direction that you're traveling, but will eventually turn off somewhere down the road. You're so nervous that you think the cop is just tailing you so you keep looking into your rear view mirror every 2 minutes. This is the "thinking" process. Then all of a sudden, you get so into watching the cop's move that you begin swerving back and forth and eventually off the road. This was the "action" that you took. Then within 3 minutes, the cop flashes on their blue lights and pulls you over. This is what the "result" of what just taken place. The cop then ask you, "Why where you serving back and forth like that?" and you give your response. Later the cop runs your license plate and your ID, then tells you that you have unpaid tickets and fines on your record. Your day has gone from bad to worst. Then he writes another citation which now not only it puts you in a position of losing money to the court system, but now it's putting you in danger of having your license revoked. This phase is the "Outcome of

Lifestyle" of the situation. Your thoughts of this cop following you had led you down the path where the situation made things worst on you than what it really was from the beginning. All these things could have been avoided only if you have changed your mindset and kept calm.

2nd Example

Let's say that you've been on your job for a while and things on your job are going well until a new employee transfers to your department. You noticed that the employee is performing much better than you are and getting more raises and promotions than you are. You starting to feel a certain kind of way towards the individual and you begin to question things. This is your thinking process. You begin asking other employees there why new people are coming in getting promotions and you've been there possibly for a long time and haven't moved anywhere? The the employees start telling you their opinions about it. You begin lashing out on the new employee. This is the "action" as in result of your thinking. Your supervisor gets wind of what's going on and calls you in the office. The supervisor begins to ask you what's going on. You begin to tell the supervisor what's going on, but things goes completely wrong. You begin to get upset and you cause a scene which resulted in a termination. This is the "Outcome & Lifestyle" you have created out of chaos. Instead of sitting down and talking things out in a calm and collective way; you made a decision to act out and make a scene. All these things can be avoided only if you learn to change your mindset.

There are so many things that I can list, but you have to learn that your thinking, the actions, and choices that you make really do affect every aspect of your life even when it comes down to choosing your friends. For example; if you hang out with 9 "broke" folks or anyone that are nothing but a bad influence in your life; there is a great possibility that you that you will be the 10th one. The reason being is that their mentally and philosophy either has or will corrupt your mind and beliefs, thus putting you in a position to become what your friends and other are around you.

1 John 3:7-8 (KJV)

7 Little children, let no man deceive you: he that doeth
righteousness is righteous, even as he is righteous.

8 He that committeth sin is of the devil; for the devil
sinneth from the beginning. For this purpose the Son
of God was manifested, that he might destroy the
works of the devil.

Proverbs 1:10 (KJV)

10 My son, if sinners entice thee, consent thou not.

1 Corinthians 15:33 (KJV)

33 Be not deceived: evil communications corrupt good
manners.

This has become my philosophy though life when it comes to finding the right friends to be around.

"If you decide to make a real change in your life and want to make an impact your peers and those around you, do so. If you can't change your friends, then change your friends."

This means if you can't change your friends, then get new friends that's on the exact level that you want to be at in life or those with similar level of thinking. You can't be in an environment that's going to keep you bounded if you're trying to be in a total different place in life. Start breaking free right now and go after your God-given purpose.

Breaking the "Glass Ceiling" Of Your Mind

I have a philosophy when it comes to breaking the "glass ceiling" or shall I say the limitations of our mind. Our minds are like a car. The next time you get into your vehicle, take a closer look at the speedometer. Depending on the vehicle you have, your speedometer will display 0-140 or 180 mph at the max. There is a device on all vehicles that controls the speed of the car called speed limiters or "governors." With these devices implanted in your car, you can only go up to a certain speed. If you were to take your car to a mechanic and have them to remove the "governors" off your vehicle, you would be able to push your car to the very limits and beyond. You will have to learn and master your thoughts. The "limited thinking" can be removed from your mind and spirit only if you choose to step out and do things that you've never done before. You will never reach your full potential in life if you have a "glass ceiling" mentality.

SKY ABOVE ME
EARTH BELOW ME
FIRE WITHIN ME

Chapter 9:
Claiming Back Your Birth Right

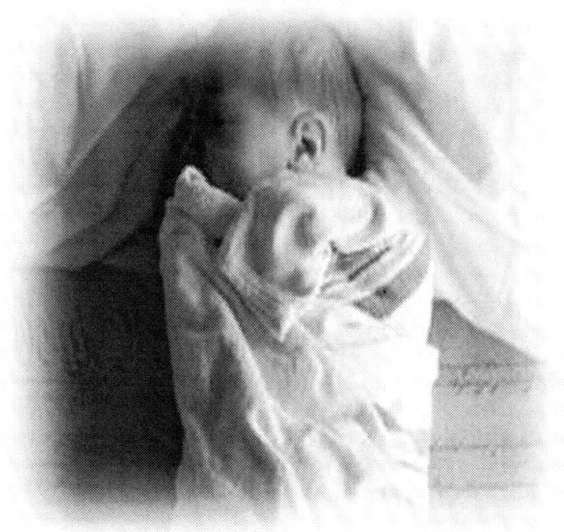

God's Vision for Your Life

Let's begin by looking at everything all around us. The reason why most of us are in the situations that we're in, especially when everything in our lives look gloomy is mainly because we don't really know what's God's plan for our lives is. Like I stated from the very beginning of this book, we're so caught up in the daily grind such as our careers, family life, and other recreational activities that we lost touch on why we're here and our true purpose. There is a divine plan for each and every one of us that was mapped out from our Creator and our Heavenly Father Jesus Christ. If it wasn't so, none of us would ever been formed or born for that matter. We all were formed and made with very unique and special talents, abilities, and characteristics that cannot be duplicated or replicated in any form of way. What we've all been given serves as a purpose here on Earth to make a contribution to the entire world. That's why it's very vital that we use our God-given abilities to share with everyone that we come in contact with and beyond.

(MINDSET OF A BELIEVER)

If you truly want to know what makes the real difference between those that win in life and those that sit on the sidelines watching people win comes down to having vision, purpose, the faith, and determination. In order to succeed past limitations, you must have first the vision. Once the vision is crystal clear, then from that point it all boils down to believing in that desire and having the will power to stick it out regardless of the situation. Your situations can do either two things: They can make you, or they can break you.

The importance of having the vision is that you're able to see the end before you even go through or begin the entire process of forming the dream. I want you to keep this in mind at all times; our Lord knew all of us before we were ever conceived.

Jeremiah 1:5 (KJV)

5 Before I formed thee in the belly I knew thee; and before thou camest forth out of the womb I sanctified thee, and I ordained thee a prophet unto the nations.

Isaiah 44:2 (KJV)

2 Thus saith the LORD that made thee, and formed thee from the womb, which will help thee; Fear not, O Jacob, my servant; and thou, Jesurun, whom I have chosen.

Ephesians 1:4 (KJV)

4 According as he hath chosen us in him before the foundation of the world, that we should be holy and without blame before him in love:

This proves in black and white that we were not just some random accident or the result from the "luck of the draw."

You might not ever understand why you're here on Earth or you might have felt for some time that you're parents wasn't prepared to have you. Whether or not it was from a financial standpoint, mentality prepared, or just bad timing in their lives it didn't matter. Either way, God was ready to have you. Just know this in your heart as you begin to go further in this book, you were chosen to be here on Earth by God. Be happy and rejoice because today is the beginning of a new day.

The Blueprint (Genetic Make Up) Of You

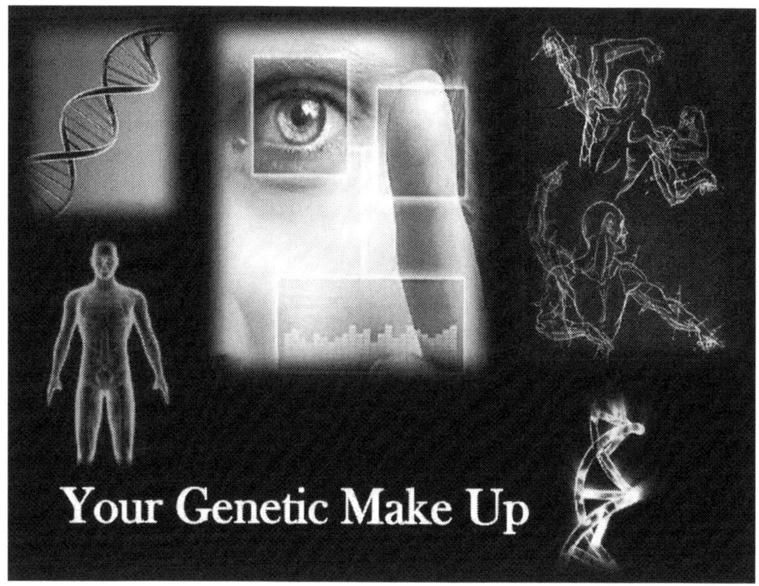

When God began crafting and forming us in our mother's womb, He outlined and chose every single detail of our bodies. He chose our race, the pigment of our skin, our hair, and every other feature. He custom-made our bodies just the way he wanted it to be in every single way. When He gave all of us breathe in our bodies, He gave a very piece of Himself in all of us. He gave each and every one of us talents and uniqueness of our personality. According to

Psalm 139:14-18 (KJV) it's states this:

Psalm 139:14-18 (KJV)

14 I will praise thee; for I am fearfully and wonderfully made: marvelous are thy works; and that my soul knoweth right well.

15 My substance was not hid from thee, when I was made in secret, and curiously wrought in the lowest parts of the earth.

16 Thine eyes did see my substance, yet being unperfect; and in thy book all my members were written, which in continuance were fashioned, when as yet there was none of them.

17 How precious also are thy thoughts unto me, O God! how great is the sum of them!

18 If I should count them, they are more in number than the sand: when I awake, I am still with thee.

All of us were made for a reason. He decided our life down to the pinpoint of our birth, how long we would live, all the way down to when we all will die. He planned the days of our life in advance. ***Psalm 139:16*** states this plainly,

"Thine eyes did see my substance, yet being unperfect; and in thy book all my members were written, which in continuance were fashioned, when as yet there was none of them." To strongly emphasize this; God saw each and every one of us before you was born and scheduled each and every day of your life way before you even breathe your first breath. Every moment of your life has been recorded in your Book whether you know it or not.

God even knew where we would be born at and where we would live according for his purpose. Our nationality and race were no accident. He molded us and shaped us without leaving any detail out. Let's take a very closer look in ***Acts 17:26***.

Acts 17:26 (KJV)

26 And hath made of one blood all nations of men for
to dwell on all the face of the earth, and hath
determined the times before appointed, and the
bounds of their habitation;

According to this scripture, he made every nation and he predetermined the time set for them and the exact places on Earth where they should live.

.

The 12 Tribes Of Israel

Tribe of Judah (African Americans)	Tribe of Ephriam (Puerto Ricans)	Tribe of Manasseh (Cubans)	Tribe of Benjamin (Jamaicans/West Indians)
Tribe of Issachar (Mexicans)	Tribe of Levi (Haitians)	Tribe of Naphtali (Hawaiians/Samoans)	Tribe of Reuben (Seminole Indians)
Tribe of Zebulon (Panamanians/Columbians)	Tribe of Asher (Brazilians/Argentinians)	Tribe of Simeon (Dominicans)	Tribe of Gad (North American Indians)

Matthew 10:6 (KJV): But go rather to the lost sheep of the house of Israel.

Zephaniah 2:1 (KJV): Gather yourselves together, yea, gather together, O nation not desired;

John 8:32 (KJV): And ye shall know the truth, and the truth shall make you free.

If we also go into ***James 1:18 (KJV)*** which states:

18 Of his own will begat he us with the word of truth,
that we should be a kind of firstfruits of his creatures.

We clearly see that God was thinking about all of us before he even made the world. This gives all of us the reason why God created it. He designed Earth and the environment so we all shall live in it. We are the center point of his love and His most valuable asset of all his creation. This is the very exact moment that we should be proud and walk in His glory. What a wonderful God we serve.

Chapter 10:
Finding True Love

Trying To Find Love in All the Wrong Places

I believe in my heart that every person deserves love or at least experience true love for once in their life. We're all trying to find that one special person that's going to make our life much better and bring out the very best in us as well as bringing out the best in them. To some, trying to find that special someone has been nothing but a complete "nightmare" to say the least. I can honestly say that it has been for me.

All I've ever wanted when it came to love is finding someone that loved me for who I am. At one point in my life, it seems like I can't even get that much. Through my personal experience, I've dated all kinds of women from all different backgrounds. Unfortunately, none of these relationships worked out. I was trying to find a good quality woman that I would think would be a perfect match for me, but noticed that I wasn't turning to God for the help. I was going by fleshly desires instead and was getting hurt time after time through the entire process. There was even times where I've even said to myself, "The heck with this dating crap. I'm better off alone."

True Love God's Way

When someone talks to me or if I hear anyone mentioning what's the true meaning of true love, a particular song comes to mind. The song "Tainted" sung by the hip hop group Slum Village that featured Dwele comes to my mid. In the outro, Dwele sings this verse "True, oh, I know true love is hard to find. Just let it find you for real. If you found love to keep it real." When I truly think about finding that special one in my life I can call my wife, I think about Adam and Eve. I wanted the type of woman that would overlook my faults or weaknesses and see nothing but my heart and greatness from within. When you find someone like that, that's when you know you have someone special. I believe in my heart that when Eve was presented to

Adam, he didn't second guess anything because he also knew from within that she came from him and that she was his equal and his partner. They both did not care that they looked like on the outside.

Genesis 2:21-25 (KJV)

21 And the LORD God caused a deep sleep to fall upon
Adam, and he slept: and he took one of his ribs, and
closed up the flesh instead thereof;

22 And the rib, which the LORD God had taken from
man, made him a woman, and brought her unto the
man.

23 And Adam said, This is now bone of my bones, and
flesh of my flesh: she shall be called Woman, because
she was taken out of Man.

24 Therefore shall a man leave his father and his
mother, and shall cleave unto his wife: and they shall
be one flesh.

25 And they were both naked, the man and his wife,
and were not ashamed.

My thoughts about love are this. Love is patient, love is kind, love is everlasting, love is enduring, and love will never hurt you in any kind of way. When someone truly loves you; they will go through the ends of the Earth to be with you and only you.

The reason why I say love is enduring is mainly because just like anything else, it's a process. It takes a lot of work and energy to truly make love work especially in a relationship. I want you to think of love as gardening. When it comes to love, it takes time, work, and great patience. You have to continue sowing and continuing watering your "seed" until you start to see your seed crack through the ground and start blooming into a flower that will ultimate bear a harvest. Through time to time, there will be weeds (Trials) that will grow in your garden (Love Life). It will take work, patience, and perseverance to make it work in any relationship. As seasons come and go, we must replant (renew our relationship towards one another). I do strongly agree that true love takes a great amount of work in the beginning. Ultimately you will experience a great deal happiness and excitement that will seem unimaginable. This is the very type of joy only God can provide.

Love That Comes With a "Special Combo"

I know that I've mentioned many times about love, my personal desires, and the breakdown on what love is from a biblical standpoint or at least how love supposed to be. I wanted to take the time to shed some light on the issue of dating someone with ADD/ADHD. In general, dating can be a very frustrating process. When it comes to dating someone with the disorder, it's a whole another challenge by itself.

I look at the entire process of dating like football. The main goal is go through the pre-season (1st stage), then through the regular season (2nd stage), then to the division

(Engagement), then ultimately to the Super Bowl to finally wear the championship ring (wedding ring). Unfortunately, I don't even make it out of Training Camp. Even if I do manage to get through the early stage of getting to know each other, I don't even make it to a second date majority of the times. Reasons could vary, but I strongly believe that impulsiveness and boredom could be the main contributing factors.

The reason that I can say impulsiveness could be one of the main factors is because of my previous experiences. Even in everyday life outside of dating, I've been notorious of doing things or saying things without thinking twice about it. It seems like the "norm" to me, but to others it poses as a serious issue. My impulsiveness in the past has ruined friendships, got me fired from several jobs, caused heated feuds, and even destroyed relationships with women.

To get a clear picture of this kind of behavior, let's use an example of a door. Most people have a door in their brains that is shut. Before most people say or do something, that door sits for a minute. For a person with ADD/ADHD, that door is either broken or just isn't there at all.

The Infamous Trap: Parent/Child Dilemma

During the entire time of dating, I've tended to go after older women that don't have ADD/ADHD or (non-ADDers). Reason being is that women without the disorder are more organized and can manage things a lot better. Usually, it would work only for a short while. In the very end, 99% of the time it results in a major disaster. My guess is that during the relationship, the roles switch from being partners to becoming more of a "parent/child" style relationship. What I mean by that is this; the non-ADDer partner would play the role of the parent while the person with the disorder (ADDer) would take on the role as a child with the "You're not the boss of me." mentality.

It's already bad enough that I felt "rejected" and "looked over" in life in general because of the disorder, but when you add this to the mix; it make things very depressing and a feeling of hopelessness sits in. Throughout my years of dating, here are some of the things that women have said to me.....

- *"I have to smoke 20+ packs of cigarettes a day being with you."*
- *"Hello! Are you even paying attention to anything I say?"*

- *"Sometimes I feel like I'm raising another child. I don't have time for this."*
- *"What's wrong with you? Are you "slow" or something?"*
- *"I feel so sorry for you. You will never have anyone in your life being like this."*
- *"I feel like I'm talking to a brick wall sometimes."*
- *"I give up! I can't deal with this any longer."*
- *"The only woman that will ever be in your life is your mother because no other woman wants to deal with you. You're better off marrying her instead."*

These are just a few of the things said over the years. There has been many times and even now where I even said to myself, "Do I even belong in the arena or is this "dating thing" even for me?" I know it's a sad and very emotional situation to be in being that nobody ever took the time to learn about the disorder before taking things to the next level. I felt like if most of these women that I've dated had actually taken the time to read a topic on "How to deal with people with ADD/ADHD in relationships" things would have gone a little bit better.

Pictures of What ADD/ADHD Look like In Relationships

Chapter 11:
The Real Challenge Begins

The Long Road to Success Begins

The way that I was treated in society was almost similar to someone that has a felony on their record. It's been five years since I had employment, almost two years since I had a car in my name, never been on my own before because I mostly stayed with family or been moving around here and there. I knew that it was time for a change and I mean "A Real Change." Another challenge was that I'm in a town with hardly any opportunity so yes this was a great obstacle for me. I almost gave up completely and even said, "I can't fight no more. I just don't have the strength to carry on much longer." I was so upset and discourage about things that I literally just wanted to end it all, until God stepped in once more. A woman by the name of Ramona Allen, who is the property manager at Eastbrook Apartments, started talking to me.

She began asking me this, "Who are you going to listen to? As a matter of fact, who has more power and authority; God's word or people's opinions? I replied back by saying, "Jesus Christ of course." Then she went on to say this, "According to the Bible, God didn't give man a spirit of fear. He gave man the spirit of power, love, and a sound mind.

2 Timothy 1:7 (KJV)

7 For God hath not given us the spirit of fear; but of power, and of love, and of a sound mind.

This means having authority and the power to change your circumstance and influence others, show love and compassion, and gain self-control. God didn't make you "slow or retarded." All of these negative things that folks said about you are nothing but a straight devil's lie. That's what's wrong with folks these days. They think they know everything and judge people by what see, but completely fail to understand anything because folks so conformed to their way of thinking." Then she went on to tell me a story about her son and how he was diagnosed with ADD/ADHD and yet people labeled him. He overcame the trash talk and made people out to be the liars they are. She then began to tell me that if her son can overcome that, I can overcome this. It's time to stand up and be bold like King David and fight back, but this time around, use the word of God to fight back. Once I gained true knowledge of myself, I've began my battle that very same day. The next following day, I went to my medicine cabinet and immediately threw away my medicine that was helping me manage my ADD/ADHD. I did this because I was so tired feeling like a "zombie" and wanted to break the "enslavement mentality" to be so dependent on the medicine. I rather learn how to manage it without the use of any medicine.

To me, this is the very first step of breaking this "enslavement mindset." I wanted to fill my head with God's wisdom, His discipline, and follow His path only. Reason being is that we've all seen the results of following other people's advice and we've all seen where that leads to which is usually a dead end. This is my own saying which became one of my mottos; *"THE WORLD TRIED TO CURSE ME AND GAVE ME DOPE; GOD LOVED ME AND GAVE ME HOPE."*

The "Trump" Card

I began each and every morning just praying and seeking God for guidance and a peace of mind during the process. As time progressed, I happen to run into a couple that told me about North Carolina Vocational Rehabilitation, an organization that helps people get employment especially for those that have a disability. At first, I kept saying, "There's nothing wrong with me. I didn't want that label being put on me. The couple began to tell me more about it what The North Carolina Vocational Rehabilitation actually do. Being that I have ADD/ADHD, to them it's considered as a learning disability and I would qualify for the help needed to regain the skills needed to enter the workforce again plus I would be provided with transportation to get you back and forth to work. I started to wrestle with this idea for a while. Being that I have no more options at that point, I was at the point where I just said, "I got to make it by any means necessary." It seemed like the very same diagnosis that was hindering me in society became the very same thing that ended up helping me in the end. I guess what I'm trying to say here is that being diagnosed with ADD/ADHD has become my "trump card" when it came to fighting back against all odds and fighting the world.

I went down to the place to ask for help to get my life together. I spoke to one of representatives there who ended up assigning me a case worker. I have to say the entire process was very lengthy to say the least. After it was all said and done, I did qualify for the assistance. They provided me a job coach to help me get my life back together and to help me get back into the working world again. The only issue that I did have with them was that my job coach was applying for positions that "they or she" thought it was suited for me which was very low pay and didn't work as much. I've saw one particular company that I wanted to work for that did pay great and would allow me to get my life back on track quickly as far as getting my very own transportation, better clothes, and my very own place. Despite what they though, I took the initiative and went after it anyway. I simply told them, "I don't care if you guys think it doesn't fit me according to what your test says, I will prove you wrong and make it work for me." I guess my King David personality came out and they was so shocked, but what can they say? So they allowed me to apply for it, but it was through a temp agency.

You have to truly understand this, everyone must start somewhere. I knew in my heart God has great things ahead of me, I just had to simply believe and walk into my destiny one step at a time.

When I went down to the temp agency to apply for the position that was listed, one of the workers there put me in contact with the lady that done the recruiting. As she looked over my resume, she began to question my work history. She asked me this, "Why do you have so many gaps in your employment history?" I've heard and seen people get denied employment due to many large gaps in their employment history. I simply told her this, "I've been living in this town for a long time and always been overlooked and over shadowed. Nobody gave me a fighting chance. All I kept getting is a bunch of negativity and put downs for all my troubles. I did everything in my own power to leave this state and moved to Kentucky in hopes of starting over and not go through the negativity I've faced in North Carolina. Come to find out that I was facing the exact same treatment that I was facing in North Carolina. I moved again to Maryland to see if I will ever catch a break. Unfortunately, I never even had my chance. I ended up back in North Carolina, which I feared coming back to because I knew in my heart I would get the very same treatment that I've always had. What happened next even shocked me. I've believed in my heart that God must have touched the woman's heart because she just had nothing but compassion, sorrow, and was in a state of shock and felt so bad at everything that has happened to me in my life. She wanted to find something for me and it's so happened that they had a position just came available to me. She gave me a hug and told me this, "I don't want you to leave North Carolina again without me helping you." Then she asked me, "Have I've done anything dealing with sanding?" I told her, "No, but I'm able to learn it." The lady reply back, "Ok, that sounds good. There's a company in Swepsonville, NC that manufactures lawn mowers and they're in need of a person in the die cast department. I will get you out there right away." I was very cheerful that she went out of her way to make sure I got the job there. I clearly saw the hand of God move in my life because I went from nothing and now this was the very beginning of getting things back in my life.

No Guts/ No Glory Pt.1

When I was given my assignment to go on 3rd shift to work in die cast, it was an experience I tell you. Being that I haven't worked in a long time, I had to get my body back used to working the graveyard shift. Besides getting use to the hours, I had to get use to the job itself. When anyone works in die cast, just be prepared to handle the hot heat and getting dirty every single day. Then to top that off, my job was to sand down the parts, which ended up having to go home with my hand being numb every single night from the power tool that I was using on the job for eight hours straight. I decided to transfer out of the die cast department after being there for almost a month to the machining department working 2nd shift. I called the machining department "The Will Grinding" department because the fact you're working 6-7 days every single week. Being that I was working those many days and being on 2nd shift had made my personal life very challenging. I spent more time there than I have at home. In my situation, I didn't mind because I needed the money to help get my life back on track. Now before things started getting better for me I was facing challenges on top of challenges ever since I started working there.

My 1st Challenge

The first challenge I've faced was getting back and forth to work. When I started working at the company, I had the transportation van giving me rides back and forth from work. Luckily, the agency that was helping me get employment was paying for the services. This allowed me to get enough money saved up to put down a down payment on car. Everything was going fine for a while until later in the month of October of 2013. The government had shut down for a short period of time and all agencies that was either receiving federal funding or state funding was not getting any funding for the period of the shutdown. Many independent businesses that were contracted through the government were not getting paid. When I was warned about it, it really hit me like a ton of bricks. Then I started to turn to God and said this, "God you didn't bring me this far to leave me hanging like this. You brought me out of a place of hopelessness and despair. I'm hanging onto your every word and I will not cease praying and seeking you Lord. I know in my heart that you will somehow provide the way to keep me going and not allow me to go backwards in my life." After a few days, the transportation van came by my apartment and picked me up for work. I was shocked that they've done it, but I was very thankful that they came by. As I was on my way to work, the driver told me this, "God must have been on your side because we were not supposed to have picked you up. Somehow you fell under another program that allowed us to continue our services. Consider yourself blessed because many people don't get this type of break. We had to refuse services for others due to the shutdown but you were saved somehow." I just began to shout because God answered my prayers and I still had my job there.

The Real Battle Begins (1-on-1 with the Devil)

With everything that has taken place in my life, I can truly say that the fight I'm continuing to fight isn't a physical battle or a mental battle. The fight I'm facing is a spiritual fight. ***Ephesians 6:12*** explains it plainly.

Ephesians 6:12 (KJV)

[12] For we wrestle not against flesh and blood, but against principalities, against powers, against the rulers of the darkness of this world, against spiritual wickedness in high places.

In order for me to truly win in this game called "Life" one must understand who the real players are, how this game is being played, and what's truly at stake. One thing I know for sure is that the Devil was doing all he can to hinder me from discovering my divine purpose here on Earth. I had to really understand every weapon he was using against me. Throughout the entire time of living on Earth, there were people that tried to ruin and sabotage my entire life, speak bad omens on my life, even tried to convince me that I didn't belong here on Earth and that I'm worthless. The Devil tried to turn everything I love and my passion against me. He had church members, friends, women, people from the jobs I worked at, my situations, even society itself to turn against me.

All these traumatizing things that were happening were the Devil trying to take me out. I had to literally "stand my ground" and place in my spirit that I'm not going to let the Devil win. I had to remind myself why I'm here and know that God is with me. He never left me or going to allow me to fall prey to the Devil's attacks. This was a fight that I'm going to win at all cost.

My Affirmations

"I'm not going to allow people's opinions or pieces of paper dictate my future. God's thoughts, plans, and vision for me are way higher than man's thoughts for me."

My 2nd Challenge

The second challenge that I was facing was the harsh criticism and discrimination from the employees there on the job. It's already bad enough that I've dealt with this a majority part of my life and to go through the exact scenario all over again is very, very frustration to say the least. When I first began in machining, I started out assembling valves and springs on the barrel part of the lawn mower. After being on the barrels for months, I was moved to several different areas within the department. During the course of the time being in machining, I was seeing other people that were working at the company shorter than me as a temp getting hired on. I was just a floater doing various jobs, but it wasn't leading me to any positions that would help me get hired on. In my heart, I knew I deserved much better than what I was getting but just wasn't given the chance. I just couldn't figure out why I was being overlooked or overshadowed to say the least. I wouldn't found out that answer for a while. I just kept on doing what I was told to do until I got moved to "cranks" where they make the crankshafts. I stayed in that department for a while and was doing very good there being that all I would is load the lines and help out in areas where needed to assist the machine operators. I was asked several times from different people this question, "Have anyone approached you about getting hired on yet?" I simply said, "No and I just don't understand why because I hardly ever missed a day, always been on time, and done everything they have asked me to do without question. I just don't get it at all." It even shocked some of the people there and they saw that I was a very hard worker, but was just being ignored. A few months later, my question finally got answered. Someone approached me and began sharing with me what they've overheard. This person was pissed off, but at first was afraid to tell me because they thought I would get irate and start fighting the employees. The person began to tell me that the reason why they're ignoring you is because they think you're "slow" and won't catch on. This person also mentioned that if that was the case, you've would've been at home collecting "government checks." The person who told me this gave me some advice on how to handle this situation. This is what was said "In this place, you gotta stand up for yourself and show these people that you can handle any task given to you. Don't let these people discourage you in any kind of way. Start fighting back and prove these people wrong." I was upset about what went down, but I had refused to give up and let these people win. I wanted to prove everyone wrong in that place, and I know I can. It was just simply a matter of time before I got my shot.

No Guts/ No Glory Pt.2 (3rd Challenge)

As I kept on working in the "cranks" department, I mentioned to some of the machine operators that I wanted them to show me the ropes about how to operate a CNC Lathe machine. I never in my life knew anything about operating a machine or went to school to learn how to operate a CNC lathe, but like anything else in life, I was willing to learn. At first, the operators were hesitant about the idea, but then they quickly saw a very strong desire that I had within me to learn more. At that point, they started teaching me little by little. They started me off teaching me how to fill up oil and what types of oil each machine took as well as filling up the coolant for the machines. Then they began showing me how to fill out the daily production sheet. They were doing all of this while the supervisors were watching. They also showed me how to clear alarms on the machines as they came up from time to time. Each alarm had a certain sequence and I had to remember how to clear them and how to start up every machine because each machine had a different function. As I kept on learning and having some real hands-on experience on the lathe machines, the supervisors were paying very close attention to what I was doing and began asking one of the operators did they think I had what it takes to run the CNC lathe machines. One of the operators said this to the supervisor, "I believe in my heart at the rate he's going, he will outperform us on the machines. At that time, they kept a very close eye on me while I was doing my job. A month later, I was approached by one of the lead supervisor and he asked me this simple question, "Do you think you have what it takes to become a machine operator? I told him this, "Yes. If these operators can do the job, I can too." He said, "That's what I wanted to hear. Your official training starts now. There is full-time spot that just opened up and you got to be on point. This is your foot in the door." I simply told him, "All I needed was a shot. Give me an opportunity and time, and I will learn how to run the CNC lathe machines.

Prevailing Against All Odds

One of the machine operator's by the name of Richard started training me. As he started training me, I learned many things about him personally. One of thc things that I quickly learned about him was that he was in the military. Secondly, he was very good with math. Third, he was also diagnosed with ADD. When he first started training me, he told me off the gate that he was going to push me very hard and be very strict on me only because he wants me to succeed and surpass him. He also told me some of the things that were being said about me also. Some of the things that were being said about me did hurt me, but I learned to use all those hurtful words as motivation to prove people wrong, not just on the job but in life. He said that the reason that he wanted to train me personally was because the fact that he saw that nobody wanted to give me a shot. He didn't like the harsh words that were being said about me and he wanted to prove these people wrong by training me. It made me realize that not only I was there to do my job to provide for myself and my family, but use the skills learned and the discipline learned from my training to help become a much better me. One thing I learned is that "military training" is the best way because if anyone have ever been in the military, when you get off the bus and onto those yellow footprints, that's where the tearing down process begins. You have to be torn down first and then begin building up their way. This was the exact way how my trainer trained me. I started learning everything that I needed to know about the CNC lathe machines from tool changes, resetting alarms, adjusting drills, troubleshooting, make adjustments to the machines, and fill out the paperwork. I must say that it hasn't been an easy road. They also had another person that was being trained as well during the time I was in training. In fact, this person was the very first choice that the leads chose to train first before me. The guy had a four day start over me and had more experience than I have. I didn't care because I said to myself that I was going to learn the lathe machine no matter what.

During the entire training, I did start out doing well. The first I was pushed to the max was within 5 days of training; my trainer got sick and went home early. I had to quickly step up and run the lathe machine by myself. I was saying to myself, "Oh Lord, why did I have to be the one this happened too? I only had 5 days of training under my belt and I don't have much experience on running the machines by myself. Why o' why Lord has this gotta happen to me right now?" I do have to admit that I was in a state of panic, but then I quickly remembered that I'm not by myself. I have support of people here and I know that they're not going to let me fail. As soon as I gain composure of myself, I started running the lathe machines myself for the first time and I had a great night. Everyone was proud of me that within a short amount of training, I managed to stick it out and prevailed. When my trainer Richard came back, everyone told him the good news that I've done an awesome job running the CNC lathe machines. He congratulated me, and told me keep it up and let's continue on where we left off.

A couple of weeks into the training, things didn't go well for me. When I was running the machines, some of my parts were out of specs according the company standards. When parts go out of spec, they are considered bad parts and usually are trashed. I had more rejects than we're allowed per day which very much frustrated my trainer. This didn't just happened just once, it kept happening on several occasions. After so many mistakes being made on my part, he started questioning himself, "Did he make a terrible mistake training me?" From his point of view and from a few others, they didn't think I could cut it as a machine operator. He even came up to and told me, "I've seen your performance, it's terrible right now. I need to know right now do you feel in your heart that you cannot handle this job. I need to know right now because if you can't, we can call this whole thing off and I will tell the supervisor that you can't cut it because I'm not going to put my name on the line and you're messing up like this." I told him; just give me one more chance to get it right. During the conversation, I was also approached by another person by the name of Christina. She was there to give me some words of encouragement to stick it out no matter what. After I told my trainer to give me another chance, he then said ok, but things got real. With every adjustment I've made, he went behind me to check my quality of my work to make sure everything was in spec according to the company. This time, I was on point with everything. I started getting faster with my checks and tool changes. My numbers started increasing dramatically. When I first started out in my training, I was only producing 700-800 parts per night. Afterwards, I started producing numbers in the thousands per night but it wasn't production. The company wanted us to produce 1,167 parts per shift. My trainer started sharing with me tips on how to hit high numbers and reduce down my downtime which helped me out a great deal. I started seeing dramatic results in quality and in my numbers. One of my best weeks with the help of God and my trainer, I surpassed the production record and done over 1,400+ parts which ended up setting a new record on the CNC lathe machines. I started gaining the respect of many people at the company and I went from the laughing stock to "The Man" on the job. I proved a lot of people wrong especially the lead supervisors there. What I was so proud about was the fact I did the job without relying on medication, I didn't listen to the lies and let them hinder me, I gave it my all, and I had the mental fortitude to stick it out and never quit. I had endured it all and prevailed. The guy that was training with me had given up the position of becoming a machine operator because he thought it was too tough. I out performed him which was incredible. This has put me in position get hired on full-time with the company. Christina was so proud of me that I didn't quit and stuck it out through the good, the bad, and the ugly. One particular night, she came by and gave me a hug and said, "Job well done. I knew you had what it takes to be a machine operator."

Golden Opportunity From Within

We all have gotten to a point in our lives where we say to ourselves, "Is this all there is to life?" I know I have. As a matter of fact, I've said that so many times especially during my "lean time." My definition of "lean time" is when you go through life depending on God to lead you on the right path and help break obstacles that seems impossible to reach your divine purpose. During my trials in life, I would sit back and began questioning things that were taking place in my life and was very unsure of what direction I should take. On one particular raining day in

Burlington, I was sitting in my Cadillac in the parking lot of a laundry mat near my apartment just thinking about everything and what I had going for myself and just felt depressed.

(All Washed Up Coin Laundry in Burlington, NC)
Ironically "ALL WASHED UP" very much described how my life was until God stepped in and turn things around for me

The reason that I was so depressed was the simple fact that I wasn't truly fulfilling my purpose in life. I knew in my heart that I deserved so much more and was destine to make a huge contribution here on Earth. I just didn't know what my purpose was. I had made a phone call to a very my best friend and sister's mom Della. We've began to talk and I told her everything that was going on with me during the entire time of my life, plus the experience that I had faced in all areas of my life. She begins giving me some really great advice about life. She told me this, "You have come mighty long way. Look at everything that you've accomplished so far. You gotten a job and was able to stick it out despite what people's opinion about you. You've prove everybody wrong in that place." She even went on and reminded me of the trials that I've overcome that most people would think is impossible. What she said to me would be what I consider to be my "breakthrough moment." She told me this, "With everything that you've endured and everything that came your way, you should write a book." It took me a minute for that to sink in, but I did agree with her the idea of writing a book. Then from there, she went on to say this, "You have a story to tell and there are literally many people out here that has no direction in life and many of those people have gave up on life. Your story could be the very thing people need to hear and read to gain their faith back and find Christ to be delivered." Once this idea had hit my spirit, my feeling and attitude immediately started to shift towards getting this book created. I started to feel really excited about my life for a change because I finally get to do something that's meaningful and fulfilling. I knew in my heart when people begin to read my story and learn how God changed my life and turn everything around for me, it would give people the hope and the faith needed to push them to their divine purpose and follow Jesus Christ. I also realized that by making this move, I have the possibility to see and experience things in life that I've never thought imagined.

At this point in my life, it was ***"MY TIME TO SHINE."***

Chapter 12:
My Time to Shine

THIS IS
YOUR TIME
TO SHINE

Do what you love,
the rest comes.

My New Direction

One thing that I can truly say about life is that it tends to have a very weird and complex way of guiding you into the direction that you need to go. The entire process of going from the "bottom of life" to becoming a writer or book author is a huge hurdle to cross. When I began this journey, I had absolutely no idea how I was going to do it or had a way to put this book idea together. All I had to start out with was an idea, the memories in my head, and a one page sheet of paper that my mother used to write about my life. I went back and mentioned the idea to Ramona about being a book author and also asked her for advice about the direction of the book. She was so delighted in the idea that I was writing a book and even knew in her heart that my book would one day touch the lives of thousands of people. She mentioned to me this, "You have an incredible story to tell. Folks tried to label you, discredit you, speak these bad omens on your life, and even tried to hinder you. To God be the glory, not only you proved these people wrong but you bounced back from all the afflictions that folks try to do to you."

She also gave me some sound advice on how to write the book. She became like a counselor to me. I have to personally say that she was a lot better than most of these psychiatric and other counselors that I've dealt with for many years. In fact, she was the reason why I was able to break free from the "enslavement pills" these doctors and psychiatrics tried to put me on. Ramona also began to ask me about the name of the book. I told her, "that I don't have a name yet, but will be working on it." She starts giving me names that would be a great book title and I've also had some names I was running through her as well. All the names that we were coming up with were all great titles, but in my eyes it wasn't going to work. Those titles that we both came up with just didn't "jump off the page" or basically it wouldn't connect with anyone that was looking for a good inspirational book to read. If I was going to give a good name for this book, it had to be something that's bold, straight forward, and basically tells the story from the very beginning. It had to be a name that anyone around the world can relate to and something that will always stick to people's heads. It took me some time to really come up with a great name of the book. I started thinking about everything traumatic event that ever took place in my life and just thought about who was there for me. Through everything I've faced, my mother was there by my side. More importantly, God was there and He never left me. I even was saying this to myself, "My mom has done a great job raising me my entire life, but it was God who made and molded me into the man that I am today." When I stated that, this immediately became the title to this book. I knew that when people would see this book and read everything that's in it, they would also see the same thing that I've seen when they read about my life and my transition.

My New Journey as a Book Author

I have to admit, I never expected to ever become an author. To be quite honest with you, I didn't think I could ever write a book. Just the mere thought of writing a book had literally made me nervous. The thing about becoming a book author is that it helps me connect with other people out there that are searching for new ways to enhance their lives for the better. It also gives me the chance to be very creative and share my views on issues that truly matters most. Though my eyes, becoming a book author gave me a sense of hope and joy in my life. It just somehow felt very right because I'm giving many readers something that is truly missing and what is very much needed in the world that we live in today which is hope, love, and the faith to move towards our destiny. I can truly say that if I didn't begin my career as a book author, my life would be very empty and full of hopelessness and despair.

Chapter 13:
My Final Thoughts

Why Did I Write This Book?

The main reason that I wrote this book because I wanted to reach out to those that felt like society had turned their backs on them or is feeling like the devil is trying to bring and tear people down. Initially, I began writing for the sole purpose of getting a lot of frustrations off my chest. This became somewhat of an outlet for me. Throughout all of my life; I've been lied to, cheated on, abandoned, rejected, ridiculed, misunderstood, shunned, ignored, and overlooked. I was so fed up with all the negativity that I was receiving and I needed a way or an outlet to fight the world back. Instead of using "fists" I learn to get my frustrations out by using words. I wanted people to view the world I came from and see all these things and truly understand my pain, but also witness my triumphs. I want people to see through my incredible story that despite everything that life threw at me, I never gave up or gave into the lies and deception. The reason that I gave this book the name "Mama Raised Me, God Made Me" was because throughout my entire life, the two most important beings in my life that really was nothing but a huge inspiration and support in my life was my Lord Jesus Christ and my mother. Without them, I couldn't have made it this far. One thing I will always remember is what my mom said to me. She said this, "If the world doesn't show you the love you deserve or give you a fighting chance, just know in your heart that I love you and God loves you too. He will never reject you or leave you. He's always there for you." Every time I think about what she said to me always lift my spirit up and helps me keep on pushing for greatness.

Nehemiah 8:10 (KJV)

10 Then he said unto them, Go your way, eat the fat, and drink the sweet, and send portions unto them for whom nothing is prepared: for this day is holy unto our LORD: neither be ye sorry; for the joy of the LORD is your strength.

This became my way of life. From that point on, I learned how to depend solely on God for the answers of life's problems that I was facing. I even said this while living in Burlington, North Carolina," I don't care what happens to me. One thing is for sure was that I was not going back to the very same place that I've left. When I left my hometown of High Point, North Carolina, I'm going to do whatever it takes not to go back home with my head tucked between my legs and prove those people right. It's either "Go Big or Go Home" and I'm sure as heck wasn't going back to High Point ever again as far as living there.

I also wrote this book to encourage others to help find their purpose in life. The real sad truth is that many people don't even know why they are here to begin with. We all have been bombarded with ideas and beliefs that society, our peers, family members, counselors, teachers, or other people that are influential in our lives try to indoctrinate in us. The only problem with the advice or beliefs that is shared with us of what we should be doing in life may not be the plan that God has paved and predestine for us in life. Let me break this down a bit further. Let's say you're planning to go to a certain place in New York.

You get in your car with a couple of friends and you start driving. You notice that you don't know exactly how to get to it or what you need to help you get to New York for that matter. All you did was get in the car and started driving in hopes that your friends will guide you all the way there, but you quickly realize that they don't even have the slightest clue on how to even leave out of the state. You ended getting lost and asking people that you come across directions on how to get to point B from point A. We all know from experience that when people sometimes try to give us direction to get to a certain place, it's not always 100% accurate. So you get the directions only to find out that they're not correct and now you're further off your destination than before. So what do you do at this stage? You either get out your GPS system or you go out and seek someone who is more knowledgeable about the area you're in and ask for assistance to get you back on track to where you need to be. The Bible is a clear example of your own spiritual GPS system in this life.

Do you know the terminology of "sign posts?" Here is the clear definition of sign posts. By book definition, sign pots are signs that point or give you certain instructions to follow. This would normally relate to traffic signs, but can also be applied to life as well. The devil will try anything he can to turn us away from our purpose in life whether that is using people or our current circumstances. Keep in mind that this is the point where we must put on the "Armor of God" and use the Word of God to fight the devil ongoing attacks and prevail. Putting on the "Armor of God" came from ***Ephesians 6:11***.

Ephesians 6:10-17 (KJV)

10 Finally, my brethren, be strong in the Lord, and in the power of his might.

11 Put on the whole armour of God, that ye may be able to
stand against the wiles of the devil.

12 For we wrestle not against flesh and blood, but against
principalities, against powers, against the rulers of the
darkness of this world, against spiritual wickedness in high
places.

13 Wherefore take unto you the whole armour of God, that
ye may be able to withstand in the evil day, and having
done all, to stand.

14 Stand therefore, having your loins girt about with truth,
and having on the breastplate of righteousness;

15 And your feet shod with the preparation of the gospel of
peace;

16 Above all, taking the shield of faith, wherewith ye shall
be able to quench all the fiery darts of the wicked.

17 And take the helmet of salvation, and the sword of the
Spirit, which is the word of God:

Your Spiritual Armor

Romans 13:12 (KJV)

12 The night is far spent, the day is at hand: let us therefore cast off the works of darkness, and let us put on the armour of light.

Jeremiah 46:3-4 (KJV)

3 Order ye the buckler and shield, and draw near to battle.

4 Harness the horses; and get up, ye horsemen, and stand forth with your helmets; furbish the spears, and put on the brigandines.

1 Corinthians 14:8 (KJV)

8 For if the trumpet give an uncertain sound, who shall prepare himself to the battle?

Take Your Stand

Luke 21:36 (KJV)

36 Watch ye therefore, and pray always, that ye may be accounted worthy to escape all these things that shall come to pass, and to stand before the Son of man.

Malachi 3:2 (KJV)

[2] But who may abide the day of his coming? and who shall stand when he appeareth? for he is like a refiner's fire, and like fullers' soap:

1 Corinthians 10:12-13 (KJV)

[12] Wherefore let him that thinketh he standeth take heed lest he fall.

[13] There hath no temptation taken you but such as is common to man: but God is faithful, who will not suffer you to be tempted above that ye are able; but will with the temptation also make a way to escape, that ye may be able to bear it.

Jude 1:24 (KJV)

[24] Now unto him that is able to keep you from falling, and to present you faultless before the presence of his glory with exceeding joy,

James 4:7 (KJV)

[7] Submit yourselves therefore to God. Resist the devil, and he will flee from you.

The Belt of Truth

Ephesians 6:14 (KJV)

14 Stand therefore, having your loins girt about with truth, and having on the breastplate of righteousness;

Isaiah 11:5 (KJV)

5 And righteousness shall be the girdle of his loins, and faithfulness the girdle of his reins.

Exodus 12:11 (KJV)

11 And thus shall ye eat it; with your loins girded, your shoes on your feet, and your staff in your hand; and ye shall eat it in haste: it is the LORD's passover.

1 Kings 18:46 (KJV)

46 And the hand of the LORD was on Elijah; and he girded up his loins, and ran before Ahab to the entrance of Jezreel.

Ephesians 4:25 (KJV)

25 Wherefore putting away lying, speak every man truth with his neighbour: for we are members one of another.

John 4:24 (KJV)

24 God is a Spirit: and they that worship him must worship him in spirit and in truth.

Colossians 3:8-10 (KJV)

8 But now ye also put off all these; anger, wrath, malice, blasphemy, filthy communication out of your mouth.

9 Lie not one to another, seeing that ye have put off the old man with his deeds;

10 And have put on the new man, which is renewed in knowledge after the image of him that created him:

2 Thessalonians 2:10 (KJV)

10 And with all deceivableness of unrighteousness in them that perish; because they received not the love of the truth, that they might be saved.

The Breastplate of Righteousness

Philippians 3:9 (KJV)

9 And be found in him, not having mine own righteousness,
which is of the law, but that which is through the faith of
Christ, the righteousness which is of God by faith:

Isaiah 59:16-17 (KJV)

16 And he saw that there was no man, and wondered that
there was no intercessor: therefore his arm brought
salvation unto him; and his righteousness, it sustained him.

17 For he put on righteousness as a breastplate, and an
helmet of salvation upon his head; and he put on the
garments of vengeance for clothing, and was clad with zeal
as a cloak.

Exodus 28:15 (KJV)

15 And thou shalt make the breastplate of judgment with cunning work; after the work of the ephod thou shalt make it; of gold, of blue, and of purple, and of scarlet, and of fine twined linen, shalt thou make it.

1 Kings 3:9 (KJV)

9 Give therefore thy servant an understanding heart to judge thy people, that I may discern between good and bad: for who is able to judge this thy so great a people?

Psalm 94:15 (KJV)

15 But judgment shall return unto righteousness: and all the upright in heart shall follow it.

Proverbs 2:7-8 (KJV)

7 He layeth up sound wisdom for the righteous: he is a buckler to them that walk uprightly.

8 He keepeth the paths of judgment, and preserveth the way of his saints.

Standing on the Gospel

Ephesians 6:15 (KJV)

[15] And your feet shod with the preparation of the gospel of peace;

Romans 10:15 (KJV)

[15] And how shall they preach, except they be sent? as it is written, How beautiful are the feet of them that preach the gospel of peace, and bring glad tidings of good things!

1 Corinthians 15:1-4 (KJV)

[1]Moreover, brethren, I declare unto you the gospel which I preached unto you, which also ye have received, and wherein ye stand;

[2] By which also ye are saved, if ye keep in memory what I preached unto you, unless ye have believed in vain.

[3] For I delivered unto you first of all that which I also received, how that Christ died for our sins according to the scriptures;

[4] And that he was buried, and that he rose again the third day according to the scriptures:

Galatians 5:16-17 (KJV)

[16] This I say then, Walk in the Spirit, and ye shall not fulfill the lust of the flesh.

[17] For the flesh lusteth against the Spirit, and the Spirit against the flesh: and these are contrary the one to the other: so that ye cannot do the things that ye would.

Romans 8:5-13 (KJV)

5 For they that are after the flesh do mind the things of the flesh; but they that are after the Spirit the things of the Spirit.

6 For to be carnally minded is death; but to be spiritually minded is life and peace.

7 Because the carnal mind is enmity against God: for it is not subject to the law of God, neither indeed can be.

8 So then they that are in the flesh cannot please God.

9 But ye are not in the flesh, but in the Spirit, if so be that the Spirit of God dwell in you. Now if any man have not the Spirit of Christ, he is none of his.

10 And if Christ be in you, the body is dead because of sin; but the Spirit is life because of righteousness.

11 But if the Spirit of him that raised up Jesus from the dead dwell in you, he that raised up Christ from the dead shall also quicken your mortal bodies by his Spirit that dwelleth in you.

12 Therefore, brethren, we are debtors, not to the flesh, to live after the flesh.

13 For if ye live after the flesh, ye shall die: but if ye through the Spirit do mortify the deeds of the body, ye shall live.

Isaiah 52:6-7 (KJV)

6 Therefore my people shall know my name: therefore they shall know in that day that I am he that doth speak: behold, it is I.

[7] How beautiful upon the mountains are the feet of him that bringeth good tidings, that publisheth peace; that bringeth good tidings of good, that publisheth salvation; that saith unto Zion, Thy God reigneth!

The Helmet of Salvation

Isaiah 59:16-17 (KJV)

[16] And he saw that there was no man, and wondered that there was no intercessor: therefore his arm brought salvation unto him; and his righteousness, it sustained him.

[17] For he put on righteousness as a breastplate, and an helmet of salvation upon his head; and he put on the garments of vengeance for clothing, and was clad with zeal as a cloak.

1 Thessalonians 5:8 (KJV)

[8] But let us, who are of the day, be sober, putting on the breastplate of faith and love; and for an helmet, the hope of salvation.

Psalm 140:7 (KJV)

[7] O GOD the Lord, the strength of my salvation, thou hast covered my head in the day of battle.

Colossians 1:18 (KJV)

[18] And he is the head of the body, the church: who is the beginning, the firstborn from the dead; that in all things he might have the preeminence.

1 Corinthians 2:16 (KJV)

[16] For who hath known the mind of the Lord, that he may instruct him? but we have the mind of Christ.

Philippians 2:5 (KJV)

[5] Let this mind be in you, which was also in Christ Jesus:

1 Peter 4:1 (KJV)

[1] Forasmuch then as Christ hath suffered for us in the flesh, arm yourselves likewise with the same mind: for he that hath suffered in the flesh hath ceased from sin;

2 Corinthians 10:3-5 (KJV)

[3] For though we walk in the flesh, we do not war after the flesh:

[4] (For the weapons of our warfare are not carnal, but mighty through God to the pulling down of strong holds;)

[5] Casting down imaginations and every high thing that exalteth itself against the knowledge of God, and bringing into captivity every thought to the obedience of Christ;

Ephesians 4:14-16 (KJV)

[14] That we henceforth be no more children, tossed to and fro, and carried about with every wind of doctrine, by the sleight of men, and cunning craftiness, whereby they lie in wait to deceive;

[15] But speaking the truth in love, may grow up into him in all things, which is the head, even Christ:

[16] From whom the whole body fitly joined together and compacted by that which every joint supplieth, according to the effectual working in the measure of every part, maketh increase of the body unto the edifying of itself in love.

The Sword of the Spirit - The Word of God

Isaiah 49:2 (KJV)

[2] And he hath made my mouth like a sharp sword; in the shadow of his hand hath he hid me, and made me a polished shaft; in his quiver hath he hid me;

Hebrews 4:12-13 (KJV)

[12] For the word of God is quick, and powerful, and sharper than any two-edged sword, piercing even to the dividing asunder of soul and spirit, and of the joints and marrow, and is a discerner of the thoughts and intents of the heart.

13 Neither is there any creature that is not manifest in his sight: but all things are naked and opened unto the eyes of him with whom we have to do.

2 Corinthians 6:7 (KJV)

7 By the word of truth, by the power of God, by the armour of righteousness on the right hand and on the left,

Psalm 149:4-6 (KJV)

4 For the LORD taketh pleasure in his people: he will beautify the meek with salvation.

5 Let the saints be joyful in glory: let them sing aloud upon their beds.

6 Let the high praises of God be in their mouth, and a two-edged sword in their hand;

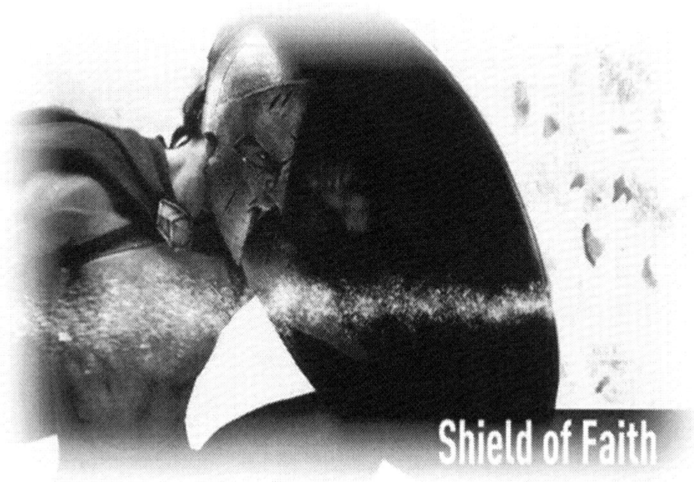

The Shield of Faith

Ephesians 6:16 (KJV)

16 Above all, taking the shield of faith, wherewith ye shall be able to quench all the fiery darts of the wicked.

Psalm 35:1-3, 9 (KJV)

1 Plead my cause, O LORD, with them that strive with me: fight against them that fight against me.

2 Take hold of shield and buckler, and stand up for mine help.

3 Draw out also the spear, and stop the way against them that persecute me: say unto my soul, I am thy salvation.

Psalm 35:9 (KJV)

9 And my soul shall be joyful in the LORD: it shall rejoice in his salvation.

Psalm 3:2-3 (KJV)

2 Many there be which say of my soul, There is no help for him in God. Selah.

3 But thou, O LORD, art a shield for me; my glory, and the lifter up of mine head.

1 Peter 1:5 (KJV)

[5] Who are kept by the power of God through faith unto salvation ready to be revealed in the last time.

Psalm 33:20 (KJV)

[20] Our soul waiteth for the LORD: he is our help and our shield.

1 Timothy 6:12 (KJV)

[12] Fight the good fight of faith, lay hold on eternal life, whereunto thou art also called, and hast professed a good profession before many witnesses.

1 John 5:4-5 (KJV)

[4] For whatsoever is born of God overcometh the world: and this is the victory that overcometh the world, even our faith.

[5] Who is he that overcometh the world, but he that believeth that Jesus is the Son of God?

Proverbs 30:5 (KJV)

[5] Every word of God is pure: he is a shield unto them that put their trust in him.

Be Strong in the Lord, By the Power of Grace

1 Corinthians 16:13King James Version (KJV)

[13] Watch ye, stand fast in the faith, quit you like men, be strong.

2 Timothy 2:1 (KJV)

2 Thou therefore, my son, be strong in the grace that is in Christ Jesus.

Ephesians 3:7 (KJV)

[7] Whereof I was made a minister, according to the gift of the grace of God given unto me by the effectual working of his power.

2 Corinthians 9:8 (KJV)

[8] And God is able to make all grace abound toward you; that ye, always having all sufficiency in all things, may abound to every good work:

Colossians 1:11 (KJV)

[11] Strengthened with all might, according to his glorious power, unto all patience and longsuffering with joyfulness;

Philippians 4:13 (KJV)

[13] I can do all things through Christ which strengtheneth me.

The Battle is The Lord's

1 Samuel 17:47 (KJV)

47 And all this assembly shall know that the LORD saveth not with sword and spear: for the battle is the LORD's, and he will give you into our hands.

Deuteronomy 20:3-4 (KJV)

3 And shall say unto them, Hear, O Israel, ye approach this day unto battle against your enemies: let not your hearts faint, fear not, and do not tremble, neither be ye terrified because of them;

4 For the LORD your God is he that goeth with you, to fight for you against your enemies, to save you.

Psalm 18:32-35 (KJV)

32 It is God that girdeth me with strength, and maketh my way perfect.

33 He maketh my feet like hinds' feet, and setteth me upon my high places.

34 He teacheth my hands to war, so that a bow of steel is broken by mine arms.

35 Thou hast also given me the shield of thy salvation: and thy right hand hath holden me up, and thy gentleness hath made me great.

Zechariah 4:6 (KJV)

6 Then he answered and spake unto me, saying, This is the word of the LORD unto Zerubbabel, saying, Not by might, nor by power, but by my spirit, saith the LORD of hosts.

Romans 11:36 (KJV)

36 For of him, and through him, and to him, are all things: to whom be glory for ever. Amen.

"Stand Strong, Face Your Fear, & Conquer Your World"

Why Do I Care For You?

In the world that we live in today, there are literally thousands upon thousands of people that really in need of a real spiritual "Faith Lift." I don't know your personal story; but I know from a mental and spiritual standpoint, I can relate. My job here is to assist you in giving you the hope, the faith, and the love that it will take to help you persevere against all the challenges, heartaches, disappointments, failures, fears, and any other obstacles that life may throw at you by sharing with you my story and the Word of God. I can make a real educated guess that some of you may have been abused or currently facing abuse in some type of way whether it was mental, physical, emotional, been raped or molested, ignored, put down, prejudged, slandered, ridiculed, abandoned, hated on, and so forth. But I'm here to tell you the very exact thing that my mother told me which is this, "I love you dearly and so does God." Even though we've never physically met yet and I hope we will one day, I hope that you will finally experience joy, peace, and love that you've been longing for through this book.

God's Love Letter to You

This was a letter that I've stumble across online a while back. This letter is for you. This letter that you're about to read clearly proves how much God values you. By the time you read this letter, you can rest assure that you will never experience this kind of love ever, not even from your parents or loves one.

God's Love Letter Addressed to You

My Child,

You may not know me, but I know everything about you ***(Psalm 139:1)***. I know when you sit down and when you rise up ***(Psalm 139:2)***. I am familiar with all your ways ***(Psalm 139:3)***. Even the very hairs on your head are numbered ***(Matthew 10:29-31)***.

For you were made in my image ***(Genesis 1:27)***. In me you live and move and have your being ***(Acts 17:28)***. For you are my offspring ***(Acts 17:28)***.

I knew you even before you were conceived ***(Jeremiah 1:4-5)***. I chose you when I planned creation ***(Ephesians 1:11-12)***. You were not a mistake, for all your days are written in my book ***(Psalm 139:15-16)***.

I determined the exact time of your birth and where you would live (Acts 17:26). You are fearfully and wonderfully made ***(Psalm 139:14)***. I knit you together in your mother's womb (***Psalm 139:13***). And brought you forth on the day you were born ***(Psalm 71:6)***.

I have been misrepresented by those who don't know me ***(John 8:41-44)***.I am not distant and angry, but am the complete expression of love ***(1 John 4:16)***. And it is my desire to lavish my love on you ***(1 John 3:1)***. Simply because you are my child and I am your Father ***(1 John 3:1)***.

I offer you more than your earthly father ever could ***(Matthew 7:11)***. For I am the perfect father ***(Matthew 5:48)***. Every good gift that you receive comes from my hand ***(James 1:17)***.

For I am your provider and I meet all your needs ***(Matthew 6:31-33)***. My plan for your future has always been filled with hope ***(Jeremiah 29:11)***. Because I love you with an everlasting love ***(Jeremiah 31:3)***.

My thoughts toward you are countless as the sand on the seashore ***(Psalms 139:17-18)***.And I rejoice over you with singing ***(Zephaniah 3:17)***.

I will never stop doing good to you ***(Jeremiah 32:40)***. For you are my treasured possession ***(Exodus 19:5)***.

I desire to establish you with all my heart and all my soul ***(Jeremiah 32:41)***. And I want to show you great and marvelous things ***(Jeremiah 33:3)***. If you seek me with all your heart, you will find me ***(Deuteronomy 4:29)***.

Delight in me and I will give you the desires of your heart ***(Psalm 37:4)***. For it is I who gave you those desires ***(Philippians 2:13)***. I am able to do more for you than you could possibly imagine ***(Ephesians 3:20)***.

For I am your greatest encourager ***(2 Thessalonians 2:16-17)***. I am also the Father who comforts you in all your troubles ***(2 Corinthians 1:3-4)***. When you are brokenhearted, I am close to you ***(Psalm 34:18)***.

As a shepherd carries a lamb, I have carried you close to my heart ***(Isaiah 40:11)***. One day I will wipe away every tear from your eyes ***(Revelation 21:3-4)***. And I'll take away all the pain you have suffered on this earth ***(Revelation 21:3-4)***.

I am your Father, and I love you even as I love my son, Jesus ***(John 17:23)***.For in Jesus, my love for you is revealed ***(John 17:26)***. He is the exact representation of my being ***(Hebrews 1:3)***. He came to demonstrate that I am for you, not against you ***(Romans 8:31)***.

And to tell you that I am not counting your sins ***(2 Corinthians 5:18-19)***.Jesus died so that you and I could be reconciled ***(2 Corinthians 5:18-19)***.

His death was the ultimate expression of my love for you ***(1 John 4:10)***. I gave up everything I loved that I might gain your love ***(Romans 8:31-32)***. If you receive the gift of my son Jesus, you receive me ***(1 John 2:23)***. And nothing will ever separate you from my love again ***(Romans 8:38-39)***.

Come home and I'll throw the biggest party heaven has ever seen ***(Luke 15:7)***.I have always been Father, and will always be Father ***(Ephesians 3:14-15)***.

My question is…Will you be my child? ***(John 1:12-13)*** I am waiting for you ***(Luke 15:11-32)***.

Love, Your Dad

Almighty God

ENDLESSLOVE
ROMANS 8:37-39
Dear God you are the HOPE that keeps me trusting
With God all things are possible
Matthew 19:26

Chapter 13:
Conclusion

My Message to You

As you can see, I could have easily given up and fall prey to all the lies, deception, the bad omens, and all the false prophecies that people try to place in my spirit. I could have accepted those lies as truth and continue to live a life full of fear. I even came so close to accepted it as "reality" and stay in that state of bondage, but I chose not to. I knew in my heart I had the potential to become great, but I had to make the decision within myself to seek the truth of who I really am. I thought about all my friends that stood by my side and believed in me when I was rejected by society. Those people reminded me of how great I was to them and the potential that they saw in me. My friends never looked at my failures, short comings, my faults, or anything like that. They only saw the very best in me. Out of those friends, I had only a few that really pushed me to become the man I am today. God has a sure fire way to bring out the very best out of a person whether it's placing them in an uncomfortable situation to make a person push themselves past their limitations or put certain people in your life to help bring it out of you. Great examples of this kind of motivation would be a drill sergeant hammering down on a cadet to help push them towards greatness, a coach pushing their players whether it's on the field or on the court pass their limitation only to help them become their very best, or a teacher in the classroom giving a struggling classmate encouragement and working with them to excel not only in the classroom; but also in life. Life had a way of doing just that for me.

Proverbs 17:3 (KJV)

3 The fining pot is for silver, and the furnace for gold:
but the LORD trieth the hearts.

Proverbs 24:10 (KJV)

10 If thou faint in the day of adversity, thy strength is small.

Proverbs 24:16 (KJV)

16 For a just man falleth seven times, and riseth up again: but the wicked shall fall into mischief.

1 Peter 1:7 (KJV)

7 That the trial of your faith, being much more precious than of gold that perisheth, though it be tried with fire, might be found unto praise and honour and glory at the appearing of Jesus Christ:

Despite everything life threw my way, I've always found the strength to not only recover from these "attacks", but to break through the limitations that was set in my mind and finally conquer my fears and adversity through faith, determination, and perseverance.

I can truly say this in many ways, I'm glad that the trials did come into my life because if these trials didn't happen in my life, I wouldn't have had the opportunity to turn to Jesus Christ for the answer, thus was led to write this book. This book wouldn't exist or even had a chance to manifest. In this crazy and corrupt world that we live in, God is all we have left to lean on for comfort and nobody else. He will only come to those that reach out to Him. You're not going to find the answer to your purpose in the things in this world. Your purpose in this life will only be answered when you go to God.

*My Circle of Influence (***BONUS***)*

I realize that in this life, you need a "mastermind" group or a group of people that's very supportive in your life. You need people that will encourage you to be the very best and also your own personal "CHEERLEADERS" in life. I have my very own "Inner Circle" which is a core group of all my friends who I call "THE FAM."

My Circle of Influence

Shawn Burkes
Teresa Hicks
Lateisha Johnson
Rey Perez
"Wassa Wassa"

Ramona Allen
Roosevelt Perkins
MY CIRCLE OF INFLUENCE
Jackson "Jax" Keomany
Nathan McAllister
Morris Jones
MY CIRCLE OF INFLUENCE

Latonja "Toot" Jones
Stephanie Reed &
Her Mother Deborah
MY CIRCLE OF
INFLUENCE
Johnny Horne
"Peaches" Horne
MY CIRCLE OF
INFLUENCE

Latrell Sanders
Rodney Poplin
My Circle of Influence
Della Jones
Candace Wilson
My Circle of Influence

Jazzy, Samarah, and Chris Jr.
My nieces and nephew
MY CIRCLE OF INFLUENCE
Shayla: Best Friend
Lesley: Best Friend
Carlos Romero & His Wife Zayda
MY CIRCLE OF INFLUENCE

David Romero
Yolanda Sanchez
MY CIRCLE OF
INFLUENCE
Titus Johnson
MY CIRCLE OF
INFLUENCE

Neashuan Philson
Thomas Dennis
MY CIRCLE OF
INFLUENCE
My best friend & homey
"JLeggs"
Tracey McCauley &
His Wife Lynessa
MY CIRCLE OF
INFLUENCE

Antonio Brutus
My best friend
Mich-lyn Cabalhim
Jasmine, Nicholas,
Katlin, and Debby
Stuckey
My Cousins
(From Top Left to Bottom Right)
MY CIRCLE OF
INFLUENCE

Tommy Rodriguez
HATERS WANTED
MY CIRCLE OF
INFLUENCE
My best friend & homey
Darius "DaBoss" Gilmore
MY CIRCLE OF
INFLUENCE

Pastor Kenny Godair
World of Pentecost
MY CIRCLE OF INFLUENCE
My brother LaDarrin Smith
Our mother Janice Smith
MY CIRCLE OF INFLUENCE

Special Thanks To....

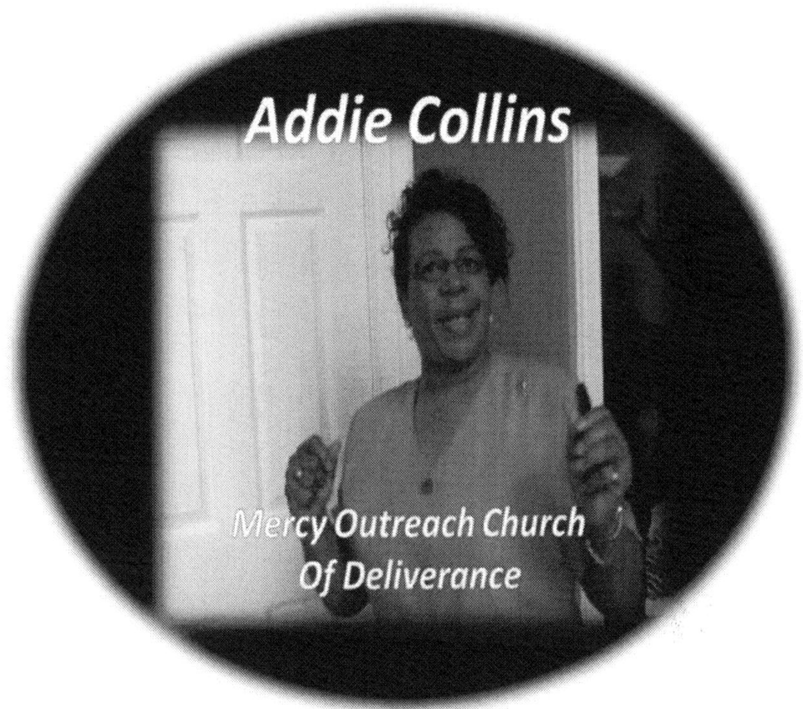

Pastor Addie Collins was one of a few that believed in me when others doubted me and never gave me an opportunity to succeed.

Reference

Adams, B. &. (1999, January 01). *Father's Love Letter*. Retrieved August 21, 2014, from Father Heart Communications: http://www.fathersloveletter.com/

Bass, E. W. (2014, June 2014). God Did It. *World of Pentecost: God Did It*. Burlington, North Carolina, United States: World Of Pentecost.

C. Outlaw, M. H.-R. (n.d.). *Role of Husband in the Bible*. Retrieved September 7, 2014, from AllAboutGOD.com Ministries: http://www.allaboutgod.com/role-of-husband-in-the-bible.htm

Fairchild, M. (2014, May 29). *Book of Esther: Introduction to the Book of Esther*. Retrieved September 02, 2014, from About.com Christianity: http://christianity.about.com/od/oldtestamentbooks/a/Book-Of-Esther.htm

Patricia, P. S. (2013, November 6). *THE POWER OF THE BLOOD LINE*. Retrieved August 20, 2014, from Christian Community Church Arklow: http://christiancommunitychurcharklow.hdpm.org/the-power-of-the-blood-line/

VanDruff, D. & L. (2014, September 27). *The Armor of God*. Retrieved September 27, 2014, from Acts: 17-11 Bible Studies: http://www.acts17-11.com/armor.html

Zavada, J. (2014, May 26). *King David – A Man After God's Own Heart*. Retrieved August 30, 2014, from About.com Christianity: http://christianity.about.com/od/oldtestamentpeople/a/King-David.htm

Zavada, J. (2014, June 04). *King Solomon - The Wisest Man Who Ever Lived.* Retrieved September 02, 2014, from About.com Christianity: http://christianity.about.com/od/oldtestamentpeople/a/Jz-King-Solomon.htm

Zavada, J. (2014, July 29). *Moses - Giver of the Law: Profile of Moses the Old Testament Bible Character*. Retrieved September 04, 2014, from About.com Christianity: http://christianity.about.com/od/oldtestamentpeople/a/Moses-Giver-Of-The-Law.htm

"We All Love You
Mama"

NOTE: The vast majority part of all scriptures verses used in this book were referenced from the website **www.biblegateway.com**

Made in the USA
Columbia, SC
28 April 2022